HANK HUNG THE MOON

HANK HUNG THE MOON

... and Warmed Our Cold Cold Hearts

RHETA GRIMSLEY JOHNSON

NewSouth Books

Montgomery

NewSouth Books
105 S. Court Street
Montgomery, AL 36104

Library of Congress Cataloging-in-Publication Data

Johnson, Rheta Grimsley, 1953–
Hank hung the moon— and warmed our cold cold hearts / Rheta Grimsley
Johnson.

p. cm.

ISBN-13: 978-1-58838-284-9 (hardcover)
ISBN-10: 1-58838-284-2 (hardcover)
ISBN-13: 978-1-60306-118-6 (ebook)
ISBN-10: 1-60306-118-5 (ebook)

1. Williams, Hank, 1923-1953. 2. Country musicians—United States—Biography.
I. Title.
ML420.W55J65 2012
782.421642092—dc23
[B]

2012001996

Design by Randall Williams
Printed in the United States of America

For Pat Grierson and Don Grierson,
both now gone, who loved Hank and began
work on a Hank book thirty years ago,

and for my husband Hines Hall,
who gave me the space, time,
and heart to finish it.

CONTENTS

DON'S STORY

I recall precisely the day Hank Williams entered my consciousness. It was January 2, 1953, the day after he died. The country radio stations were in mourning, playing nothing but Hank's songs, a lot of the dirge-like Luke the Drifter stuff. It seemed his death was the topic of every conversation.

It was my thirteenth birthday and the day classes resumed after the Christmas break at Moss Point High School, where I was a seventh-grader. During fifth-period PE class—really a sort of unsupervised recess for older boys back then; you could play football or dodgeball if you were so disposed, or you could lean against the gymnasium building and whittle, talk, and chew tobacco—I sought out Luray Gassoway.

Luray was a worldly boy of fifteen or sixteen, a grade or two behind in school, but a font of wisdom nonetheless, my hero and mentor. His family was poor, even by the standards of our Mississippi paper-mill town, and somehow I knew that Luray had endured hardship, had lived already. He was leaning against the brick wall of the gymnasium, singing "I'm So Lonesome I Could Cry," and meaning it. When he finished the song, he said, "Poor old Hank. He ain't gonna sing no more." His sense of loss was palpable.

I realized that something momentous had happened. Luray didn't say it in so many words, but I understood that Hank's songs were about what the world held in store for us. Years later, Bob Dylan said it is possible to learn how to live from Woody Guthrie's songs. Hank's, too. In the weeks and months following Hank's death, I became an avid neophyte under Luray's tutelage.

— DON GRIERSON

He spun his words around
Like planets in the universe
Of his cosmic country mind
Until they shone like stars
Brighter than the fire of his eyes.
But it was his voice, ohgod his voice,
That made the sun.

— CHARLES GHIGNA

PROLOGUE

Talk about your near-misses. Hank Williams died on one end of January 1953—New Year's Day—and I was born on the other, January 30. I can claim cosmic connection.

When I was seven, my family moved to Montgomery, Alabama. That was seven years after Hank was buried beneath a granite hat and gumbo clay in that town's Oakwood Cemetery Annex. We weren't there for the wake or the funeral, but, by god, we often stood 'round that grave.

Timing is not my strong suit. I remember lying on my back in wet Georgia grass with siblings and first cousins, studying the dome of a sky, watching for falling stars. "There's one!" my older sister would holler, always first at everything from falling stars to shaving legs. I'd have missed it, squirming around on the ground saying, "Where? Where?" The same way I missed Hank.

He fell too fast.

I've never been one to wish I had been born in a past century, or a future one. I've been happy with my own share of pianissimo memories: bubble lights on Christmas trees, flannel boards of Jesus and the apostles, sit-upons and s'mores at Brownie campouts moved inside in case of rain. I know absolutely that I came of age at a good time, the best time, with that "cushy birth" the Boomers in *The Big Chill* admit to, when "normal" parents meant one stayed at home to coddle you and another went out to bust his ass making a living to buy us stuff we didn't really need. There are a few folks from history I would have liked to say I had shared a half century with—Eleanor Roosevelt, Ernie Pyle, John Steinbeck. But I would not have wanted to share their turbulent times. I don't mind having missed the Great Depression, the Dust Bowl, and World War II.

I do mind having missed one thing.

It would have been nice, really nice, to have had a thirty-cent ticket for an unreserved seat on a hard church pew on June 11, 1949, when Hank made his *Opry* debut and wine from water, when he healed the sick of heart and did encore after encore, singing like he was born to sing. Singing like he didn't have long to get it all done. A relative few witnessed those miracles: 3,574, to be exact, give or take a few no-show ticket-holders. And the ones who were there, who touched the hem of his garment, belong to a generation fast disappearing.

I suppose it would be far worse if I *had* been around, had been alive in 1949, or '50, or any of the years that Hank was giving live performances, and had missed them, had missed him. That would have been a tragedy, or negligence of the worst order. This way it's more an error of fate. Definitely not my fault. Nothing that can be hung on me. It wasn't physically possible for me to shake Hank's hand or get his autograph or show my devotion by attending his funeral like twenty thousand of the faithful did. Born too late, that's my excuse and I'm sticking with it.

Yet I knew Hank, same as I knew my father and mother, or my grandparents, or others who worked to make my life happier and complete. I knew all my life what I'd missed, even before I could articulate that longing. I grew up with Hank a fixture in my life, a real presence, same as did most Southerners. His music was everywhere in our formative years, oozing out of honkytonks and truck stops and car radios and black-and-white television sets. Hank was true. Hank was music. Hank was life.

I remember putting on my father's stiff white cowboy hat, the cheap one made of shellacked straw. His good cowboy hat I wouldn't dare touch. I'd stand at the full-length mirror nailed to the back of the bedroom door and pretend to be playing guitar while singing, "Hey, Good Lookin'" or "Kaw-Liga." I loved Hank's novelty songs first. It would be some years before I'd need or understand his deeper thoughts.

I outgrew Hank for a while. Or so I thought. For about ten minutes in my teens I thought Hank had no relevance to my happening teen-aged life. I got too big for my britches, as my mother might have put it. Hank Williams's music became briefly like the outhouse at MaMa's, or the nasty Maxwell House can where she spit her snuff. That kind of deep country thing, all at once, began to offend my organdy sensibilities. Those objects were familiar as cricket chirps, had been there forever, yet overnight became an embarrassment. I guess those familial anachronisms left over from another age were hard evidence of an uncool genealogy best not to broadcast, or even admit to myself.

This was when I was young and oh-so careful about what the rest of the world thought of me, so young that I earnestly believed the rest of the world did think of me. The Hank Williams hillbilly sound was a bright ruby scar I hid under my sleeve.

But I remember the moment, the place, a Ford Pinto the green of baby food peas, when I shyly admitted my love for Hank Williams. Turns out, it was an abiding love. It was summer in south Alabama, one of those humid days when wisteria competes with a dead polecat for your nostrils. Wet sweat appears in perfect concentric circles at your armpits. I was twenty-two, a newlywed, a passenger in that ugly un-air-conditioned car on the highway between Mobile and Monroeville, doing a passenger's main job, searching for noise, any noise, on the radio.

Hank's voice broke out of the AM box the way Man o' War left the starting gate. That voice, Hank's voice, was startling in its intensity. Nothing prepares you for it, no matter how many times you hear it. It's always like the first time. And I had not heard Hank in a long while.

So I confessed.

"Maybe it's because he's from Alabama," I said to the young man who was my husband then, Jimmy Johnson. Jimmy had spent his childhood in the textile mill village of Lanett, and I had done most of my growing up in Montgomery, about eighty miles to the west. So he knew Hank, too, and wasn't really surprised at what I said: "I can't help it. I think he's good."

In the privacy of that Pinto, Jimmy agreed.

Let me help you get past the presumption of that conversation. You must put it in the context of 1975, and ignorance. My generation was not musically deprived or unsophisticated. Not by a long shot. But for a short while there, my schoolmates and I liked the imports, not the domestics. We were especially keen on the British; if a lead singer didn't call his fellow band members "bloke," we didn't have much use for him. We Southern youth were perfectly comfortable with Brits dressed as French courtiers singing about the Irish, but we squirmed and rolled our eyes at hearing an Alabamian in native accent whose music had a beat like that of our own hearts.

OUR GENERATION ALSO HAD the heavy-hitters, the keepers, no less than Elvis, the Beatles and Bob Dylan and Janis Joplin and Arlo Guthrie and The Who and Ike and Tina and Aretha and a list of talented musicians so long that the Sixties, even today in a new century, is still the well to go to if you need a soundtrack for a movie or lively background for an automobile commercial.

And it wasn't altogether my generation's fault that country music had become passé. After Hank's death, country for a time went to the dogs. By the early to mid 1970s, around the time of my personal Hank revival, the country music I'd grown up hearing my father play—Roots music, or "Americana" they call it now—had been replaced by an extremely tacky, quasi-pop sound that was over-orchestrated and phony and that tried without much success to straddle several genres. It was smooth and banal and decidedly un-cool. Nobody born after 1945 would admit to liking it. Nobody hip, anyhow. We were the Woodstock Generation, not *Grand Ole Opry* groupies.

And Hank? Well, Hank and all the lesser lights of his era were history. The country music scene, such as it was, anxious to be uptown, had left his kind behind. Hank's world smacked too much of outdoor privies— everyone's, not just my grandmother's—and blue collar jobs and beer drunks in the family woodpile. The quintessentially cool Ray Charles had in 1962 recorded an album of country and western music, *ipso facto*, hillbilly music, that covered many of Hank's songs. It had been a huge hit and arguably paved the way for country music eventually to become mainstream. Ray Charles's covers were instantly acceptable.

But pure Hank, Hank doing Hank, wasn't. It was yesterday, and we were all about today. It would be years before Willie Nelson would grow his red locks long and convince us strutting, know-it-all Boomers that not only was pure country acceptable, it was the *ultimate* in cool.

BUT IN THAT FATEFUL year, 1975, a little ahead of my time for my generation, I looked back. I didn't turn into a pillar of salt, simply into a Hank fan once more. We were living in Monroeville, in south Alabama where there was only one radio station in town, which played mostly country, mostly old, three-chords-and-the-truth country. I was half the staff at the *Monroe Journal*, a weekly newspaper in the county where, incidentally, Hank had lived briefly as a boy. In 1933 Hank had moved in with his McNeil cousins in the town of Fountain in Monroe County and attended fifth grade. Opal McNeil spent the year with Lillian Williams, Hank's mother, so she could go to Georgiana High School. It was an exchange student situation in a practical, rural sort of way.

Jimmy was the other half of the newspaper staff that year. We split the duties, everything from taking the big-snake pictures to writing the headlines. Often I'd be riding down the road alone, on my way to cover a boring meeting of the Excel City Council, or to take a photo of the first cotton bloom or some country woman's prize zinnias, and Hank's voice would slice through the static like a meteor through a night sky. For the first time since early childhood, Hank was riding with me. I liked it.

I hadn't realized how much I'd missed him until I heard that voice again, until its hot brand of honesty seared my heart, reminding me of what I knew deep down in places I thought I'd lost. It tugged at my emotions the same visceral way a yellow bug light on a screened porch always did when seen from a little distance. There are people under that light, eating fried catfish and swapping lies and swatting mosquitoes. It's like watching your childhood once-removed. Hank's voice was like that. It was so simple and direct and part of my past that my heart saluted even when my head marched on down the road. Hank's voice was home. He was people like me.

I thought wrongly at the time that I'd been the only Simon Peter, denying my love for hillbilly music thrice before the cock crowed. I later discovered it was a common enough phenomenon in my age group. When I met my second husband, the late Don Grierson, I knew I was hooked after he sang in a voice so close to Hank's that I felt the rock roll away. Don told me he'd gone through the same evolution. Loving Hank as a child, moving on to Elvis and folk, returning as a young adult to his original passion for true and gritty, "industrial-strength" country, as he aptly described it.

We discussed it often, Don and I, why the hell we ever took a hiatus from the music we loved the most. Peer pressure, we decided. You didn't crank up Hank when everyone else was playing Foghat. There was another reason for me: Hank's music told too much about my roots and all the dirt around them. About the way my south Georgia kin said "sturm" for "storm" and "directly" (pronounced "te-reckly") instead of "in a little while."

Hank's music told family secrets. It was far too real to be fun. Which, at that age, was what I thought all music was supposed to be.

It's the same reason young blacks don't flock to blues concerts. What black youth in his right mind rushes to embrace the musical philosophy of oppression and impossible poverty and dirt-floor shacks where nobody loves you but your mamma, and she might be jiving, too?

It wasn't possible for me to admit to loving Hank until I was past puberty, when I had enough self-confidence to love my own family, to accept my own core. It's a tricky thing, growing up, deciding what is you and what is just everybody else. Once I was free to be myself, I was free to love Hank again. The way I instinctively had when I was small, responding to the primal beat and the authentic sound. Turns out Hank was on target all along—I was the one taking the magical mystery tour.

After Don's death in 2009, it fell my sad lot to clean out a Louisiana attic in a small house where we'd spent part of each year for a dozen years. I had to sell the house; it proved too much to handle financially, emotionally, physically. When Don retired from his job as a journalism professor in Birmingham, we had hurriedly shoved personal belongings, including the entire contents of his university office, into that attic. Thrilled to be quitting, tired of academia, he, we, never even bothered to open or examine the boxes marked with the usual cryptic descriptions, flotsam from his long career.

The moving out was a lonely task. You can imagine. It was also hot as a pot of Community Coffee in southwest Louisiana, and I worked alone for several days in the stifling confines of that attic. Mostly I bounced boxes down the access ladder a rung at a time, to the ground, then to the U-Haul, deciding I'd be emotionally more able to check out their contents later.

It was the box marked "HANK" that stopped me in my tracks. I pushed that box down the ladder, too, but didn't move it immediately into the truck. I took it instead to the living room, into the artificial cool. And I opened it and sat and read and read, losing all sense of time and forgetting my deadline to get myself out of the house.

I had known the interviews existed. Don and his former wife, the late poet and professor of English Pat Grierson, had begun work on a book about Hank Williams in the early 1980s. Both Hank enthusiasts and convinced of the literary quality of Hank's work, they were approaching the task a bit differently than others had. Pat, who ended up doing most of the work, put out an "open call" to her English-professor colleagues:

> A Call for Papers, Poem and Essays on the Lyrics of Hank Williams, Sr. as Literary Achievement. Deadline: April 15, 1983. For inclusion in the Anthology Hank Williams: Poet of the People . . . Only previously unpublished works will be considered.

Don and Pat had contacted a lot of the usual country music suspects, too, and the response had been good. In that box were transcribed short interviews with Minnie Pearl, Tom T. Hall, Don Helms, Jerry Rivers, Chet Atkins, and sundry Hank kin. There also were poems and essays and short stories submitted by those who hadn't known Hank but who studied and revered his work, who put the exacting academic measuring stick to songs scribbled on the backs of napkins. There were lovely original poems by the celebrated Miller Williams and an Arkansas language professor named James Francis Ford and Alabama's Charles Ghigna (now best known as "Father Goose," a respected and prolific children's poet). There were dozens of other submissions from those who agreed with the young Griersons that Hank was the "poet of the people."

There was no book manuscript as such, just odds and ends and scraps of revisions and letters back and forth between Pat and Don who had done the work together, but mostly by long distance, after their marital separation. I think the work might have been a way to keep a hold, however tenuous, on the relationship. A Hank bond is one not easily broken.

"Bebe," Pat began one letter. "I am requesting that this poem be rejected with the opportunity for [poet's name] to write another if he wishes. I don't think it's good enough."

Every now and again in the 1990s after Don and I were a couple, Pat would visit us or we would stop by her apartment in Jackson to say hello. The two of them, who remained extraordinarily close until Pat's death a few months before his, would mention the book, even contemplate finishing it. I asked Don repeatedly why they didn't.

"Oh, I don't know," Don would say in his laid-back, humble way. "It's all over the map."

THAT MUCH IS TRUE. All over the map. The appreciations extend like the United Kingdom of Hank. Alabama relatives of Hank remember fondly their last meetings with the great man, how he brushed off his boots and went to church and sang as one with the astonished congregation. Fans who saw his first performance at the *Louisiana Hayride* ponder the momentous event. Drifting Cowboys Helms and Rivers share their world-weary road stories. Musicians who knew him, or wished they had, talk off the cuff.

A lot of the revelations are basically old news now, stories that have been told in several Hank biographies published since then. A lot of those characters are gone. Dead.

Some of my favorite unpublished submissions are terrible literature, but rate a 10 on the Richter Scale of Sincerity.

There is a poem from a Thorn Hill, Tennessee, woman, that is so astoundingly bad I cannot figure how it got into the same box with verse by English teachers and inaugural poet Miller Williams. And yet it might be more representative of those of us who love him than, say, a Miller Williams poem. She wrote: *This one's for Hank/This one's for the man/Who sang of today/And the hope of tomorrow . . .*

There was much misinformation in the box, too, due either to faulty memories or extrapolations and exaggerations. Various Hank cohorts have Hank meeting Audrey in Nashville, or Montgomery at Lilly's boarding house, or at a medicine show where Hank was performing in south Alabama, the latter being the case if you believe the more recent biographers. One friend describes Hank's second wife, Billie Jean, at Hank's funeral wearing "red, clinging pants." The photographs from that day prove otherwise. Beneath her tailored white coat Billie Jean wore black, just as Audrey did, and Hank's mother.

I don't know what Pat and Don would have done with the disparate material had they seen fit to finish the book. I just know that they, like I, loved Hank and wanted to pay tribute in the best way they could. They were a little ahead of their time in launching the project. It was before much serious writing had been done about Hank.

I understand the inertia that might have stalled them. Both had demanding jobs at universities. It's hard to give up your free time when it's limited. It's also difficult to figure a way to say something new about Hank. No less than five biographies are on my shelves, including the most recent (I think) and most lyrical one by the late, great Paul Hemphill. There also are tedious academic treatments that make you want to crawl your way to safety. On the other end of the spectrum are sensationalized accounts by rock-and-roll journalists. And there are, of course, the predictable and sometimes self-serving family memoirs.

Perhaps Pat and Don came to the same conclusion as Elvis Costello: "Writing about music is like dancing about architecture: It's really a stupid thing to want to do."

But all of us who string words together in feeble attempts to tell a story half as well as Hank, all of us think we have something to add to the legend, another way to interpret genius. Mostly we want an excuse to get closer to the music and the man. For we need Hank for something more elemental than entertainment, sometimes in an urgent way. We need him to continue to function in this life, to make sense of things, to help wrestle down demons. We need him the way the gandy dancers needed their rhythmic chants to get through a ten-mile stretch of railroad repair. The way a beautician needs bobby pins. Hank was more than our troubadour. He was, in a way, our savior.

IN WORKING THE SOUTH as a reporter and columnist for the last three decades, I've collected my own Hank stories. Seems like everyone you meet has one. It's hard to find an Alabaman past a certain age that doesn't have some encounter or memory to tell you about. I even believe some of them.

My husband Hines Hall grew up in Millbrook, Alabama, a community just outside Montgomery. Born in 1941, he learned to tell time by listening for Hank's WSFA Radio show broadcast from downtown Montgomery. It began each morning at a quarter past 11. His mother didn't approve of Hank's lowbrow style of singing, so Hines had to watch the clock himself so he'd know when Hank Williams was about to begin. Big hand. Little hand. The rest followed. And Hines has another Hank story: He once saw Billie Jean Williams in the Montgomery airport after Hank was dead and gone. Hines knew it was her when "Mrs. Hank Williams" was paged on the intercom. Exciting stuff.

One of my best friends from high school, Patsy Porter Smith, grew up in a Hank-steeped household. Her father, the late Jimmy Porter, played steel guitar for Hank in one of his early Montgomery bands. There were dozens of early band members—though their number is quickly fading now—but none more professional and devoted to Hank than Mr. Porter.

A Memphis newspaper colleague, Mary Alice Quinn, misted over when I told her my current project was a book about Hank. In her seventies now, Mary Alice remembers the exact moment, on a pier in south Alabama, when she heard her first Hank song.

One of my best friends, Luke Hall, left Burnsville, Mississippi, to seek his fortune in Memphis at age fourteen. He ended up driving a city bus, eventually becoming a bigwig in the international transit union. Luke had just as soon never hear anything but Hank Williams songs. Ever. And that somehow makes a Mississippi farm boy's story not unlike that of the Jewish Canadian poet and songwriter Leonard Cohen, born rich, who in song places Hank Williams "100 floors above me in the Tower of Song." Rich man, poor man, Indian chief. They all love Hank.

A decade ago I was interviewing a Montgomery woman who made unusual jewelry and collage art. Hank was not part of the storyline. Not at all. Not at first. She lived in a storybook cottage her father had built for her. We hit it off, the artist and I, ate Blue Moon cheese sandwiches for lunch, and then, as an afterthought, she took me to meet her father, Roy Bagley, an Ernest Hemingway look-alike who ran a Montgomery building materials salvage yard.

It didn't take long before Roy was telling me about sitting next to Hank in junior high, back when Hank was called Hiram, a kid with spectacles and no interest whatsoever in school. That's the way it goes with Southerners of a certain age.

All roads lead back to Hank.

HANK HUNG THE MOON

There Ain't No Light

Hank Williams wrote: "I saw the light,
no more darkness, no more night."
Then he said the trouble was
that there ain't no light
and he may have been right;
just as he was about other important things
like weeping robins and midnight trains.
But if it's true that there ain't no light,
not even the smallest, sanguine spark,
we're wandering aimlessly in the dark.
And I believe Hank Williams was afraid of the dark.
I am too.
How about you?

— JAMES FRANCIS FORD

CHAPTER ONE

My father was four years old when he lost his father. A mule kicked William Crawford Grimsley in the head, and my grandfather never recovered from the injuries. He died a few days later, at age twenty-nine.

About the only memories Daddy has of his father involve the death scene. Daddy remembers how neighbors blocked off the dirt road that ran in front of the family's farmhouse in rural west Georgia. This was Miller County, Georgia's southwestern edge near the Florida border, the semi-tropical, peanut-farming, mayhaw-jelling part of the state. It was bosky country, with deep topsoil and clear creeks and longleaf piney woods full of rattlesnakes and foot-washing Baptists. The Grimsleys lived near the county seat, the sleepy burg of Colquitt, a designated bird sanctuary, at least so-designated by the time of my childhood. If ever a place were destined to be a bird sanctuary, peaceful Colquitt was it.

The intent of the temporary roadblock was to detour traffic and keep the area quiet for the poor young farmer who lay dying. It's hard to imagine such a courtesy necessary. Even today there's not enough traffic to stir dust on that same road, which remains dirt.

But it seems a civilized and gracious gesture, rerouting buggies and farm wagons and the occasional pickup truck so that a family could gather around a loved one and say goodbye in private. And trust me. It would have been quiet in 1929. I know from experience. When I was sixteen, in 1969, forty years later, I spent a summer in that same house where my grandfather died, with an aunt who had just lost her husband, my father's brother, Bill. His death lingered like a morning fog in a mountain hollow. Aunt Beulah, a fierce female in many respects, was scared to live there alone, and the plan was I'd ease the transition in return for a summer job at the garment factory where she was floor supervisor.

We worked all day in the "sewing room," as everyone called it. I was a pattern-bundler, gathering up a right sleeve, a left sleeve, a bodice, a collar, trying to make "production," a management standard, production being an arbitrary, optimum number of housecoats or pantsuits that needed to be bundled in a day. We got a bonus if we made production. By night both Aunt Beulah and I were dog-tired. She'd cry herself to sleep early, and I'd study the sky through the bedroom window and wonder how I'd ever talked my way into babysitting a widow. I think I did it to impress my father, whose respect was a trophy worth hauling home.

When I became a widow in 2009, I thought a lot about that long-ago summer. I hadn't volunteered to go there strictly to be kind, understand, to help out a middle-aged woman wrestling the grief demons; I also wanted a summer job. But as friend after friend peeled away from my penumbra of gloom and depression the year after Don died, I realized that Aunt Beulah had needed me desperately. And not just because she was scared to live alone. I was just a kid, someone she could talk to all night when she wanted, and ignore when the tsunami of hurt overcame her. I was perfect for the job, and not the one that paid.

It wasn't all bad, believe me. The food was spectacular, landing, as I had, in a nest of country cooks with cupboards full of lard cans to fry anything that didn't hop out of the skillet. All my south Georgia relatives had big gardens, too, which not only provided food but made sure there were no idle hands to draw the devil onto the front porches of summertime.

I gained ten pounds. And I left with all the pantsuits I could carry.

Something else significant happened that summer. I grew to love the absolute quiet, those still nights so far from major thoroughfares. I think it is part of the reason I live in a remote area right now. Once you've heard the quiet, you cannot forget it, not if you're sane. For that kind of quiet is full of sound. Full of whippoorwills and owls and tree frogs and mysterious scuffles in piles of leaves. In that way a south Georgia night is exactly like a Hank Williams song. Dark and full. The evenings are as heavy as lighter knots, and just as aromatic. The world seems empty, but for you and your kin. You might be so lonesome you could cry, but you wouldn't change it, either. Not for all the world.

My birthplace has changed little. As late as the 2000 Census, Miller County was one of only two Georgia counties that did not gain population, but lost.

I've always thought first memories would make a good psychological study, and I'm sure there have been some such studies done. If one of your first memories is of death, the death of your own father, it has to line your soul with a sadness that won't quite go away. Ever.

For all practical purposes, as a lad Hank Williams lost his father, too. Hank was six when Lon Williams left his family for a Louisiana VA hospital after being diagnosed with a brain aneurysm. When Lon recovered after nearly a decade in the VA and made at least a half-hearted effort to return home, Hank's mother Lillian wanted no part of the man or the marriage. And though Hank, unlike my father, had the luxury of later, as an adult, re-establishing a relationship with Lon, the early departure had to be tough on a boy.

Memories like those would bedevil you all your livelong days. My first memory, on the other hand, seems, well, *juvenile* compared to my father's, and to Hank's. My first memory is of leaving my Mickey Mouse ball outside and awakening in the middle of the damp Florida Panhandle night to worry about it. I slipped out of my bed, padded through the living room and into the dark to retrieve my favorite toy. On my way back through the living room, rubber ball in hand, I thought I saw a stranger sitting in my father's new brown recliner, smoking a cigarette. I woke the entire household with an ear-piercing scream. My father came running with a gun and a flashlight.

There was nobody there, of course. Nervous and half-asleep, I'd imagined the man, who, come to think of it, bore an uncanny resemblance to my father and smoked the same brand. I simply had seen what I was accustomed to seeing.

That silly walking nightmare was terrifying enough to constitute a first memory. I never liked Mickey Mouse much after that. But the memory's trumped-up trauma pales next to my father's first, and says something significant, perhaps, about the difference in generations. I remembered a fright. Daddy remembered death.

DADDY'S MOTHER, LUCILLE, DID not remain a widow forever. Out of necessity more than love, as she vigorously and often admitted, she soon remarried and moved just down the road a piece. Her new husband's home was isolated as well, on a hardscrabble farm not unlike the one she'd left. The house, a log cabin at its core with asbestos shingles covering its even humbler roots, is the one I'd always associated with my father's growing up years.

As children, my sisters and I would use a stick to draw a hop-scotch board in the white sand just beyond the front gate, using ubiquitous, small red rocks chock full of iron as our markers. Often we'd climb the mimosa that grew just outside the kitchen window, inventing elaborate games that made good use of its powder-puff pink blooms. There were blackberries to pick all along the dirt road in the summertime, and at Christmas a poinsettia bloomed in the chimney corner. By the time we came along, it seemed the idyllic place to grow up, a cacophony of sounds and smells that blended together in some rural recipe and came out as "home."

There was the stench of hogs in their pen, not a stone's throw from the house, the better to fling the scraps. And the outhouse, which had its own vile odor, contributed to the peculiar domestic blend. Those smells mixed with heavenly ones coming from the kitchen, built separately from the rest of the house. Lucille fussed over a wood stove to prepare delicious meals, and then served them up with boundless enthusiasm, Liszt at a Steinway.

What I never realized as a child was that my father didn't really do all his growing up in that house where I spent long and happy weeks, usually in the summertime. The main thing it had to do with him, really, was that his mother lived there for sixty years. He spent some time there, of course, right after his father's death, but not as much as I had imagined. Lucille's new husband, Burl Bush, also a farmer, had three strapping boys and a daughter of his own and not much use for my father. Aubrey, as they called him, was now one of three step-children who had become Burl's responsibility to clothe and feed. Aubrey was duty, not delight.

Daddy had a solution. He marched on down the road another mile or so, spending a lot of his growing up hours at his grandmother's house, a haven for a young boy craving love and attention. He got it there. In spades. He also got spending money, certainly not the norm for the time and place—the Depression era in the Deep South. Being "adopted" by his grandmother probably kept him from being bitter or defeated or worse.

In late-night reminiscing, Daddy can describe every outbuilding on his grandmother's working farm as if he were there yesterday. At his mother's house, he never went hungry or unclothed or took beatings, nothing like that. But at his grandmother's, he was a baby, the pet. It could have been far worse.

But losing your father—and then your grieving mother's attention, as my daddy did—is still a hard psychological row to hoe. So he did what youngsters do when they've been neglected or ignored; he left home early. After finishing high school at seventeen, he struck out for Atlanta, the Big City, two hundred miles to the north, a young man determined to make it on his own and off the farm. Within a few months he had worked a series of odd jobs, sometimes more than one at once, living at a boarding house where the woman who ran it packed a sack lunch for him each morning; it was part of the deal.

One of his Atlanta jobs was at the famous Varsity Drive-In, world's largest, hustling hamburgers and hotdogs and filling the orders of Georgia Tech students who were, to say the least, on a far different career track. There was a patois for the servers and car-hops there, a lingo that began with "What'll ya have? What'll ya have?" when customers walked through the door. "Squirt one" meant pour a Varsity Orange, and "walk a dog," meant fix a hot dog to go. A "bag of rags" was potato chips, and "Yankee dog" was a plain dog with mustard.

He was still in Atlanta, working a factory job, when Uncle Sam decided Rex Aubrey Grimsley was needed. By his country. Lucille phoned the boarding house from Colquitt to relay the news. His induction center was near Atlanta, but he'd be sent for short stays to Miami Beach, Oklahoma, Birmingham, Meridian, Paris and Brownwood, Texas, Shreveport, and Seattle. He was quarantined for measles in Washington before finally he boarded the troop ship in San Francisco that would take him to the Pacific and to war.

It has occurred to me more than once that it couldn't have been all that easy being a daddy without a pattern, without some personal example to follow. My father's growing-up society was mostly matriarchal, if you don't count the taciturn stepfather. Same as Hank's world, the women ruled.

It's amazing what a good, intuitive job Daddy has done with his own four children, considering there was absolutely no playbook. If he has erred, it's on the side of thinking responsibility for his four children never ends. He had precious little parental hovering. We would get the opposite treatment. He taught mostly by example—by never missing work, by keeping his own counsel and instruction to a crucial minimum. He gave us room to fail and incentive to succeed. His only spoken advice when teaching me how to drive was delivered in an authoritative tone when I inched into a right turn: "Remember," he said. "You don't have to *stop* to turn right."

I HAVE SEEN ONLY one picture of my paternal grandfather, and he looks both intense and handsome. Daddy inherited precious few of his father's possessions but he got the intensity and the good looks. There is a wishbone tie tack on a silk tie that belonged to William Crawford that my mother had framed for Daddy one Christmas. And, of course, that "formal" photograph in which both William Crawford and his new wife look windblown and a tad desperate. The portrait could be a poster for *The Grapes of Wrath*. A tie pin and a photograph. That's about it. No land. No money. Absolutely nothing to jumpstart his life.

My grandmother would outlive her oldest son and her second husband, as well, and leave almost everything to her only daughter. My father's Army checks sent home from war in the Pacific paid for his sister's education at a teacher's college. After the war, it seemed imperative to Daddy to make a living, and he didn't return to school.

Daddy never complained. About anything, really. He had his own ways of coping in lean years, and they didn't involve therapy, of which he was skeptical, or medication, which he avoided, or whining to family and friends, which is how he would characterize heart-to-heart talks.

Somewhere in his early life he discovered that music is a cure like no other. And he's used it as such all his life, even as a boy. He speaks reverentially of his grandma's Delco generator, housed in its own outbuilding, a poor man's Golden Calf. The Delco powered the radio that played, always on Saturday nights, the *Grand Ole Opry*. The broadcast at that house was open to anyone who wanted to show up, sit quietly and listen.

Daddy wasn't the first to discover music as a balm and bandage rolled into one. Poet Maya Angelou, for instance, has called music her refuge. "I could crawl into the space between the notes and curl my back to loneliness," she wrote. Music has kept the field hands picking, the oarsmen rowing, the freedom riders riding. Music is good for what ails you.

Almost as soon as he got out of the army, in 1946, Daddy married my mother, a raven-haired, blue-eyed country girl named Betty Houston. She was born on September 17th, Hank's birthday, two years after Hank. Mother was, for a few years, a Colquitt elementary school teacher whose fiercest point of pride was—and is—that she was the first of her family to finish college.

The first piece of furniture my parents bought as young marrieds was an RCA cabinet radio/turntable combination that played 78 rpm's. As a "bonus" the furniture store gave them ceramic salt and pepper shakers shaped like Nipper, the RCA Victor dog. Mother gave the shakers to me a few years ago because she knows I admire the old radio. I checked their value on eBay and discovered that Nipper shakers are quite common and must have been popular lagniappe. I don't care. I love those dogs.

Daddy hauled the record player home in 1948, the same year Hank became a regular on the *Louisiana Hayride* and recorded "Lovesick Blues" in Ohio.

It was the year before that, 1947, when Hank and Audrey, another set of poor newlyweds from the country, boarded a train in Montgomery and headed for Nashville. The trip ended fortuitously, with Hank hooking up with Fred Rose and beginning a fateful if short collaboration that was the country music equivalent of Lewis and Clark. Together they explored uncharted territory. Already Hank was a veteran performer, touring the south Alabama roadhouses and dairy shows and county fairs. He also had his own show on WSFA Radio in Montgomery, a spot secured in his youth when he'd sing on the sidewalk outside the studio. By 1947 the show had made him a regional celebrity.

And Hank, an alcoholic since his teens, had been at least once to a Prattville dry-out sanitarium. At the tender age of twenty-four. he'd known local fame and alcoholic pain, both providing bags full of grist for his twenty-four-hour creative mill. The *Opry* was in his near future.

HANK'S MUSIC MIGHT HAVE been part of the reason that Daddy bought the record player, but not exclusively. Hank's tours and Montgomery radio appearances wouldn't have reached southwest Georgia, though the *Louisiana Hayride* broadcast out of Shreveport certainly could be heard there when the wind was blowing right. Hank became a regular on that show in 1948. Broadcast from KWKH at 50,000 watts, the *Hayride* was a live and lively, four-hour country music extravaganza that could be heard over most of the East, in fact.

But it was not until 1949 that "Lovesick Blues," Hank's first recording, would become a ubiquitous, Number One hit, blanketing not only the South, but the entire U.S. I bet it didn't take long for Daddy to go out and get that record. Never known for frivolous purchases, Daddy would have made an exception. Did make an exception. And he would have "wore it out," as we say, playing that song again and again. But a shellacked 78 record may be the most indestructible inanimate object on the face of the earth. You have to throw one on a concrete surface with some heft to break it. So I have my father's copy of "Jambalaya," with "Window Shopping" on the flip side.

Also in '49, Hank debuted on the *Grand Ole Opry*, which Mother and Daddy always listened to with their friends, especially two other young Colquitt couples: Wink and Frances, and Wallace and Dixie. I can envision the scene. Mother, with her perpetual pride in setting a proper and ample table, preparing dinner for the six of them, using as talisman her West Georgia College home economics medal that she kept in the cedar chest with other family treasures. Daddy, not home long from the butcher shop in town, smoking a cigarette and anticipating an evening built around music and good food. After supper they might play Chinese checkers at the table.

Wink and Frances eventually would divorce, as would Wallace and Dixie and, most famously, Hank and Audrey. Mother, the queen of euphemisms, still says under her breath that someone is getting "a Wink and Frances" instead of using that ugly word "divorce." So, in south Georgia parlance, Hank and Audrey got a Wink and Frances. One heard 'round the world.

But at that long-ago time in that quiet town, the couples in my story were more or less happy, breaking even and not down, planning ahead, not looking back. They were good looking and cooking. And the music moved them.

Daddy was a really handsome fellow, with dark hair and blue eyes and a thin, tall frame—a build not unlike Hank's, but without the spina bifida stoop. Grammar school friends used to tell me my father looked like actor David Jansen, TV's "The Fugitive" and if he hadn't been my father I might could have seen it. He has kept his looks, same as he kept that old cabinet record player.

He went about everything—work and play—with a vengeance. As a young father he could waterski in the Gulf, help create a school project from a cypress knee the night before it was due, win a kewpie doll pitching quarters at the fair, build a patio for our Florida house with stone and pink mortar. Pink mortar. For his girls. In his youth he drove too fast, cursed too often, smoked like old Birmingham, and wasn't always patient or progressive politically. But everything he tackled he tackled flat-out. And his passion for music was and is no exception. He can't play a note on any instrument, never could, but I've never known anyone who loved music more. It lifted him.

Today he routinely watches a taped show called *Midwest Country* on the RFD cable channel. It's out of Minnesota, believe it or not, but Daddy holds no regional bias when the music is good. His favorite part of the weekly show is when the Hank impersonator David Church takes the stage. But the show's steel guitarist fascinates him, and he knows the names of all the members of the house band.

THE OLD TURNTABLE DOESN'T work anymore, hasn't for a long time, but my parents keep it in a place of honor in a bungalow that was on their acreage before they built a new brick house. Mother puts special knick-knacks on top of it, so many that it would take half a day to lift the lid if the innards did work. The stack of records, at least the ones left after my routine pilfering on holiday visits, are stored in the bowels of a seldom-used cabinet.

There are other artists besides Hank on the records that have survived my weekend record raids and the seventeen moves of my parents' marriage. There's Tennessee Ernie Ford singing "This Old House." Talk about your sad songs. Even as a child I could envision that falling-in place, its roof with no shingles, its dying owner with no time left to fix sagging doors. A sensitive child, I wanted to save it, the house not the man. Why was Tennessee Ernie so hell-bent on dying and leaving his home? I think the loneliness of that song is in part why, as real estate tastes go, today I still prefer fixer-uppers.

There is also Tennessee Ernie's hit "Sixteen Tons," a song that proved prescient to Daddy's long devotion to one employer, a grocery company he was fiercely loyal to that eventually fired him. There's Red Foley's cover of the Thomas Dorsey song "Peace in the Valley." There's also Daddy's favorite non-Hank song, "Tennessee Waltz," the Patti Page version. When my older sister JoAnne graduated from the University of Alabama at Birmingham's medical school, an orchestra played a beige version of "Tennessee Waltz" before the ceremony. Daddy leaned down and looked at me and smiled, knowing I would appreciate the song, however anemic the version.

There's the LeFevre Trio singing "Just A Closer Walk with Thee," "Just a Pickin' and a-Singin'" by Curly Williams and the Georgia Peach Picker, "Heartaches and Flowers" by Roy Acuff and his Smoky Mountain Boys.

And there are Hank records, of course. Had to have Hank.

JoAnne was born in 1950, the year Hank really took off. He had three big hits that year: "Why Don't You Love Me," "Long Gone Lonesome Blues," and "Moanin' the Blues." My folks were still living in Colquitt, renting a house in town so Daddy would be near the meat market where he was learning the butcher trade. I like to imagine him listening to the radio while he cut meat, not singing along—he never does—but swinging his cleaver in time to the lively beat.

I read somewhere once that songs of that period were three minutes long, or less, because that's the limit to the amount of music the old 78 records could hold. That fact alone makes the Hank oeuvre impressive. That he could tell those complete and universal stories in less than three minutes and in simple language makes Tolstoy seem verbose and Shakespeare one of his own fools.

Take the song "You Win Again." It is two minutes and thirty-four seconds of narrative economy and romantic drama. It needs nothing. It wastes nothing. And it's twelve seconds *longer* than "I Can't Help It if I'm Still in Love with You," which, if it had been the only song Hank ever wrote, would qualify him as a genius and natural-born storyteller.

In a long-ago interview with Don and Pat Grierson, the poet Miller Williams, father to the brilliant singer-songwriter Lucinda Williams, talked about the quality of sound, the purity, if you will, on those old 78 records that once were my parents' pride and joy:

The voice of Hank Williams on the 78 will break your heart. And you don't hear that voice on a 33. It's a different voice altogether; they've reprocessed it, and they've reprocessed all the soul and the guts out of it. The Hank Williams you hear on a 78 will tear you to pieces. We'll play the same songs on the albums people buy now and then on the old 78; you won't believe it's the same person.

JIMMY'S PARENTS, MY LOVELY first in-laws, once had their own stack of 78s. As young boys, Jimmy and his brother Vic used them as flying targets to toss skyward when they got their first BB guns. It's a youthful indiscretion that haunts Jimmy still. And it was a terrible waste. Only a mother like theirs, the saintly Lera Johnson, would have accepted such destructive play without beating her boys to bloody pulps. But think about it. Where are the eight-tracks you once had stacked in a corner of the den? Who could know, really, that every technological advance wasn't necessarily an improvement?

The covers on the MGM Records 78s say they were "Pressed on Metrolite Non-Breakable." The fine print says, "under normal use."

I was born too late to see Hank, to hear him sing in person. And too late, if I'm honest, to remember hearing the old RCA rig play. I'm sure it still worked fine when I was a toddler, but by the time I was four or five, television had replaced the radio as the entertainment center of our household, most households. We huddled around the new black and white set at our house on Pensacola Bay to listen *and* watch the hot tunes of the day on *Your Hit Parade* with Gisele MacKenzie.

By the time I was in school, my father, like everyone else, had switched his favorite music from 78s to 33s. He simply borrowed my older sister's portable turntable whenever he wanted to hear an album. Records had evolved into albums. And he often did want to hear his albums.

On days off, which meant most weekends, Daddy would stretch out on the dark green living room sofa that seldom got used, putting his head on Mother's decorative pillows that weren't really meant for such, propping his long and narrow feet on the armrest at the other end. And he'd listen to music until he fell asleep.

He had branched out a bit since his youth, now listening to Billy Vaughan waltzes and Floyd Cramer's piano and one album, *Honky-tonk Songs,* with a sleeve I greatly admired. That one had a saloon girl in full-feathered regalia on its cover and seemed racy and dangerous. I wondered that Mother would allow it in the house. Sometimes, when he didn't have the energy to search for the turntable in the messy bedroom JoAnne and I shared, he would call out to one of us to play a little something on the living room piano. JoAnne usually got the summons as she was the more accomplished pianist, everything being strictly relative.

JoAnne would grudgingly sit and stutter through "Stardust" or "Moon River," reading from the stack of sheet music we kept in the piano stool. If I got the call, I played one of the two recital pieces I'd managed to commit to memory: "By a Blue Lagoon" or "The Cowgirl."

It didn't seem to matter what we played, or for how long. Weary off the road—Daddy was a traveling man by now, working for the Winn-Dixie grocery chain—the music put him to sleep every time, no matter the tempo or how flawed the execution. As soon as he slept, we were free to slip out and resume our games.

Because Daddy was on the road most weekdays and weekday nights, we both revered and feared him. He'd blow in on Friday afternoons, his grip fat with inexpensive or free souvenirs, like the miniature motel soaps that I loved, his eyes strained from all the driving, and Mother would report to him a week's worth of our indiscretions. I don't think he liked to punish us for things he hadn't witnessed, but he assumed it was his duty. And so he reluctantly did.

When Winn-Dixie transferred Daddy from Pensacola to Montgomery in 1960, Daddy was thirty-four, already having lived five years longer than Hank. Like many of our neighbors, we often visited Hank's grave, same as we would have a family member's. It was a destination in demand whenever Georgia kinfolks came to see the Big City sights, or simply a good turnaround for a Sunday drive. We'd most always, all of us, get out and walk around, admiring the hilltop view that "ol' Hank" enjoyed. In perpetuity.

Hank wasn't so much a celebrity in our minds as a distant cousin or close friend who had died far too soon. He spoke our language and knew our secrets and made us feel better about our troubles and foibles. He was not so much in the ground as all around, having made that successful transfer to immortal status. In our Baptist church on Easter we'd sing "Up from the Grave He Arose," but I had less trouble thinking about Hank than Jesus when I envisioned such a magical Return.

The adults called him by his first name, and always added "Ol'" in front of Hank, as if he'd been eighty-nine instead of twenty-nine when he died. "Ol' Hank," was, of course, also what Hank called himself, and we all bought it. A wise old soul, that was Hank. Whenever the adults talked about ol' Hank, they sounded happy and sad at the same time. It was a dichotomous situation, being sad about his death but enjoying the very thought of him still.

"Ol' Hank won't be singing no more songs." "Poor ol' Hank. Audrey won't torture him no more." "Ol' Hank is up in Hillbilly Heaven."

And some days, when the paycheck wouldn't stretch quite far enough, when the babies were bawling and the biscuits got burned, when Mother was fussing, or when he knew Sunday was almost over and that Monday morning he must get up, button another white starched shirt to his chin and hit the road again, it must have seemed to Daddy that Hank had had all the luck.

Ninety years without slumbering,
Tick, tock, tick, tock.
His life seconds numbering,
Tick, tock, tick, tock.
It stopped, short,
Never to go again,
When the old man died.

— HENRY CLAY WORK, FROM
"MY GRANDFATHER'S CLOCK"

CHAPTER TWO

I can't carry a tune in a bucket. Guess there's a hole in my bucket like the one Hank sang about. That never stopped me from trying to carry my share of a song. It's fortunate that public schools in my day encouraged tuneless singing. A special, visiting music teacher made the rounds, weaving her way down the hallway on stilettos, beaming a fluorescent smile at all of us expectant children tucked liked crabs into the shells of individual blond desks. Maybe she longed to be elsewhere, performing on Broadway, or at least on a stage not defined by a linoleum rug. You wouldn't have known it, though. Southern women of the early Sixties were conditioned to act like they loved whatever they were doing, whether it was ringing a doorbell with your Avon order or dishing out fish sticks in a school cafeteria. A Southern woman put her best foot forward, made lemonade from lemons, bloomed where she was planted.

And so the poor woman smiled.

This occasional music teacher brought all the necessary equipment with her, same as a carpenter brings his tools. She handed out hardback song books and sometimes, on special days, percussion instruments from a big cardboard box. We used those to form a rhythm band. In the big rhythm band box there was a triangle, a tambourine, a drum, castanets—and one year, a major musical departure from the ordinary: an autoharp just like Mother Maybelle Carter's.

You always hoped to land the triangle, which was easiest of all the instruments to play. If you scored the triangle, you sat poised to perform, knowing it was your job to bide your time, to provide punctuation, *the emphasis,* the "exclamation point!" at the end of the musical measures. You didn't have to beat yourself silly during the rest of the song.

One day the young music teacher had an inspiration and let the rhythm band march around our classroom, weaving through desks and terrariums and coat racks like a Second Line jazz funeral on Bourbon Street. It added an exciting dimension and quickly got out of control. We clearly were having too much fun. I claimed the castanets and pretended to be a flamenco dancer, not exactly in sync with the rest of the marching troupe but exceedingly happy and loose. It might be the last self-confident dancing I ever did.

I can't imagine in that day of non-air-conditioned, open-windowed classrooms that anyone on the hall got much done while we were banging and beating and bleating. But they knew the music teacher was on her way their way; it would be their turn to get down, and soon. At any rate, nobody stopped us.

FROM SECOND GRADE THROUGH sixth, I attended Dalraida Elementary School in Montgomery, a typical red brick maze of an institution ruled by women and shaded by pines. It took up a suburban block right out of Ozzie and Harriet, if Ozzie and Harriet had had a little less money and lived near an airfield. I loved the school, and felt exceedingly safe there, from morning till 3 o'clock dismissal. Patrol boy Randy Slack, who wore a crew cut all the way through high school, would whistle me across the street and into a world of Clean Plate Club buttons and thematically matching bulletin boards and high-top socks held up around your knees with rubber bands. It was a forgotten time long ago, before bullies and bullets enrolled in elementary schools, and before the music died.

Most of the time during music class, we simply sang, songs of unbelievable horror, come to think of it, considering we were such innocent kids. With imaginary banjos on our knees, we sang of being shot in the streets of Laredo and of a grandfather clock that stopped when an old man died. That particular one gave me nightmares. I always pictured my own kindly grandfather, especially when we came to the part about "his spirit was pluming his flight . . . his hour of departure had come." My grandparents had, in fact, a relentless mantel clock that was so much a fixture of their home I didn't remember it ever not tick-tocking. What if it were to stop?

Thinking back on those songs, I'm reminded of a George Jones story he tells in his autobiography. His famous hit, "He Stopped Loving Her Today," was tricky to sing, and George didn't like it to begin with. After flubbing several attempts in a recording session, he threw the music down in disgust. "Nobody is going to buy this maudlin son of a bitch," the Possum angrily, and wrongly, predicted.

Maudlin songs were part and parcel of elementary school music. There was the usual complement of Stephen Foster songs with angelic dead women and Old Black Joes. Songs about train wrecks and sinking ships, dying Confederates and lost dogs. No happy, upbeat songs for us, no sirree. Your ship sank, your dog ran away, and the Yankees won.

There was a certain ceremonial flair to the racket. The music teacher, or on some odd weeks our regular teacher, would pull a pitch pipe from her pocket, blow a single note and let the caterwauling begin. The energy we used up in those off-key renditions of campfire songs probably kept down the number of fist fights on the playground and food fights in the cafeteria. The musical disharmony encouraged civic harmony.

For several years the Flutophone was on our mandatory supply list. That meant our parents had to spring for a six- or seven-dollar, white and red plastic horn that looked an idiot's clarinet. Pitched in C, my favorite key, you could play a full chromatic scale. There was a hole at the bottom, which you covered with the thumb of your left hand when playing. You made noise by blowing softly into the red plastic mouthpiece and opening and closing the finger holes to form notes.

The Flutophone was another excellent way to wear out the student population and keep it honest. We worked for weeks on a standard like "Home on the Range," producing more spit than music. Concerted effort was the lesson, I suppose, or perhaps it was a way of identifying the kids with promising embouchures for junior high band. Or just maybe somebody, somewhere in the system, simply loved music.

You read so much about "taking music out of the schools," and I agree with those who think it is an awful idea. It's an awful idea to take music out of *any* part of life. But I'm wondering why musical parents don't volunteer their time when budgets don't allow for music sessions. Probably because they are all holding down real jobs, trying to make the rent and the Subaru payment.

But, in the 1960s, my elementary school era, there was always a stay-at-home mom—the only authorized kind then—who would volunteer to visit her child's classroom to lead songs, dance, even give a mini-concert on whatever instrument she'd learned in her own high school band. Terrell Finney's mother, our favorite guest, would wear full Native American regalia and kokopelli dance around the reading circle, popping her hand against her open mouth as if the warpath ran through the fourth-grade room. We were entranced. I don't know if she had Indian blood, or just the costume. But her performance beat the other mothers' cupcakes any day of the week.

Looking back, music followed us everywhere as children. It was on TV, in good programs like *Name That Tune* and the *Ed Sullivan Show*. The morning after the Beatles appeared on *Ed Sullivan* we wasted an entire play period discussing which was the cutest. I want to remember Paul won the vote.

Music at school went beyond the classroom, with plays, recitals, and square dances on the auditorium stage and an occasional religious record played over the crackling intercom during devotional. The week John Kennedy died, we were awash in dirges.

Music walked us home. Suddenly it was spilling out of our book satchels on transistor radios that arrived dramatically on the scene like C-rations thrown to troops from helicopters. We carried our transistors like personal packages of joy, tuning into WBAM, the "Big BAM," a 50,000-watt AM station that signed on the year of my birth and Hank's death, 1953, and reached much of Alabama, Georgia, and Florida. It was undeniably Montgomery's most popular station with all folks under thirty. Big Bam staged summer shows at Montgomery's Garrett Coliseum, the same ugly but utilitarian hall where Hank Williams had once played at the grand opening. The first live act: Hank Williams. Big BAM Shows ran throughout my childhood, with the station hosting not one, not two, but half a dozen big names for the price of one ticket.

Shows might include Leslie Gore and Paul Revere and the Raiders, the Monkees, the Grass Roots, and Lou Christie, two or three headliners all on the same night. Tickets were never more expensive than $4, but Mother heard that teenagers sometimes made out in the nosebleed seats and so we weren't allowed to go. But the mere thought of those stars hanging out in our hometown rocked us, not to mention the idea of brazen sinning near the Coliseum rafters.

Early mornings on the Big BAM were devoted to farm reports and gospel music, but popular and country music played the rest of the day. When the station powered down at night, "Dixie" was the sign-off song.

THE MAIN SOURCE FOR my music fulfillment as a girl came not at school or home, however, and certainly not from the piano lessons that we were force-fed like cod liver oil. The main musical free-for-all was at church. We sang our hearts out in the Baptist church. Later I would realize it wasn't necessarily a "joyful noise." Sometimes it was just noise. Ellyn Dudley, my high school music teacher, would use my denomination as her ultimate insult. When the Robert E. Lee High chorus that she led went wildly off-key, she'd stop us in mid-measure and moan: "You sound like a Baptist congregation Easter morning."

But I would have years of enjoyment singing in church services before I had a clue it wasn't beautiful as well as heartfelt. We had not reached, for a sweet while, what the Baptists called "the age of accountability," that vague demarcation when you no longer had ignorance as an excuse for anything. So we sang flat-out, those gloriously bloody hymns with militaristic images and nail-scarred hands. Golgotha was better and bloodier than the streets of Laredo. Beethoven once said, "To play without passion is inexcusable." And that probably covers singing as well. It's no wonder Baptist hymns are best sung around the campfire by old drunks.

I especially liked singing the maudlin but melodic invitational, head bowed and eyes closed, wondering as I sang just which sorry sinners were stumbling down the aisle to ask public forgiveness. If the blood-shedding in "Just As I Am" didn't guilt-trip you into going forward, you were hopeless and doomed. Good music, for my money, was emotional music. And it still is.

My sister and I joined the youth choir, of course—we joined every social opportunity the church offered—but choir practice was more structured singing and not nearly as relaxing as the congregational kind. I happened to come of age during the beginning of the church cantata fad, which I am sorry to report persists. Cantatas, at Christmas and Easter, meant we sang songs nobody had ever heard of, much less enjoyed. But I was in love with the choir director, Dennis Woodard, who was not handsome but winning. I would have sung Greek arias if he'd asked. Singing those stylishly difficult, minor-key cantatas was hard work. Congregational singing was far more recreational and rewarding.

By junior high Brother Woodard had selected me to sing alto in a trio he formed for special musical presentations, including summer choir tours. Judy Land sang middle soprano, and Cindy Wells high soprano. Margaret Adams played the piano for us, and we practiced at home, at the church and sometimes even in a car riding to engagements. Our trio briefly caught fire. We did a pretty snappy "Count Your Blessings" that the entire church heard, and that led to invitations at assorted secular events. We even got paid a couple of times.

The night Montgomery's new Arrowhead Country Club opened, our trio sang "It's a Wonderful World," and I, for one, certainly believed it. Hank Williams songs were passé by then, so we never included a single Hank song in our limited repertoire. But we did struggle through a lesser-known Glen Campbell song, "If You Go Away" for a church Valentine's banquet. *If you go away, as I know you must. There'll be nothing left, in the world to trust.* That had enough of the lovelorn juice to satisfy even thirsty, romantic me. By turn, each of us sang a verse before harmonizing on the chorus. I sang with such intensity when it came my turn to solo that a handsome boy named Charlie Johnson mocked me the rest of the night by screwing up his face into a tortured frown and humming.

I think I might have been at my all-time happiest performing with that Baptist choir trio, underlining with my wavering alto, if you will, the melodies that we tried to sing in tight harmony. Judy believed she should be singing soprano, not the notes sandwiched in between in no man's land, and she quit. Cindy was so good that she didn't need a church trio to secure performances. Brother Woodard got the call to a bigger church in Birmingham. The trio disbanded, but by then I was the only one who cared. I was devastated. All that training with Flutophones and castanets. All down the drain.

I've thought about excusing the much-maligned Audrey Williams at times. She couldn't sing, but she desperately wanted to. Folks in charge of the *Louisiana Hayride* even put her in front of a dead microphone to keep her happy but quiet.

"If anyone had ever doubted how truly awful Audrey's singing voice could be, they got a screeching earful when she and Hank teamed up on 'Lost on the River' and 'I Heard My Mother Praying for Me,'" Paul Hemphill wrote. "She yowled, jumped in whenever she felt like it, and practically drowned out the voice of a husband who one day would become the quintessential country singer . . ."

In a way, I feel sorry for her about the singing, or attempts at singing. Not about much else. She was a shrewd, free-spending, round-heeled, manipulative woman, and those were her good qualities. But I admit it would be hard to hang around with a troupe of hillbilly singers, especially Hank Williams, and not open your mouth. There would be something so unnatural about remaining a mom and mum; call it cruel and unusual punishment. Especially if singing meant you got to wear a grownup cowgirl suit and stand in a spotlight on a stage. It must have been tough to sit down in the audience in your civvies with the rest of the groupies while husband Hank wowed the adoring crowd, including women, lots and lots of women.

On the other hand, I've heard "Lost on the River" and the other infamous Hank and Audrey duets that make your skin crawl when she misses notes or entire keys. It doesn't help that "Lost on the River" is one of my favorite Hank compositions. Mark Knopfler and Emmylou Harris sing it on the Hank tribute called *Timeless* and you realize how beautiful, sans Audrey, that song really is. It contains the perfect metaphor, "the river of life." It's so simple and yet apt you want to slap your forehead and swear that surely somebody's used that before. Hank doesn't stop there.

Hank speaks of "old sad yesterday," and you know he's successfully shortened every description of despair ever written to just the three perfect words: Old sad yesterday. Perfect.

"Tomorrow you'll be another man's wife." That phrase packs rejection into a single sentence, again with minimalist perfection. Using both yesterday and tomorrow in turn, he crafts a perfect little song.

I'm convinced that if Audrey had kept her mouth shut, "Lost On the River" would be up there with "I'm So Lonesome I Could Cry."

But she didn't. And I didn't. I couldn't sing but it didn't stop me from trying. And trying. I joined the glee club in high school, where thankfully many voices diluted any individual impact. I loved the spring concerts when we wore evening gowns—last year's prom model—and sang for an hour, on stage and in the spotlight. I had no real business being there. But, my god, what a feeling, watching Ellyn Dudley tap her little conductor wand on the lectern, beginning the performance and fueling my dreams. I wanted to be a torch singer, one of those who wore a black strapless dress and a rose in my hair. I would lean into the microphone and almost whisper the first lyrics, "*What'll I do, when you, are far away . . .*" and the handsome Philip Marlowe-ish private detective at the back table would swoon.

I'm wiser in maturity. I sang with Don, because he pretended I could sing. I often sing on the front porch when I'm alone, and in the car driving by myself down the lost highway, when it's impossible to bother anyone else. I often sing along with Hank, but then he's certainly used to awful duet partners.

Face it. Most of us are destined for the bleachers, not the stage. We are most likely to be spectators, as the brilliant if tragic Fred Exley wrote in his masterpiece, *A Fan's Notes*. Only a few really break from the pack to lead it. And if ever we should force our way forward, forgetting our place, we'd better hope the microphone is dead. We'd better pray that sucker is unplugged.

"As I know the South, Hank Williams was an almost perfect reflection of the South . . . The South that I knew, as I understood it, was hard-bitten, a world where you could not hope to succeed, but to find something meaningful in your failure. A world in which the cards were stacked against you and there was a certain honor in playing them straight . . ."

— MILLER WILLIAMS

CHAPTER THREE

The office and recording studio is in a barn-like building on a road Norman Rockwell might have painted, only it would have been too perfect for him. Storytown Road meanders through jade middle Tennessee hills near Hartsville, northeast of Nashville. The road loops and winds through green farms that smell of fresh-mown hay, the proof of honest labor. And beyond the office-barn is a modest brown house with a red roof where Hank Williams's daughter and her husband live.

Hank's daughter. Hank's blood.

We were born twenty-four days apart, and both grew up good little Alabama girls who wanted to please. Cathy in Mobile, I in Montgomery. I guess that's why I have this presumptuous notion that I know Hank Williams's daughter, the one they sometimes call his "lost daughter." She wasn't lost at all. Just hidden for a while in a bureaucrat's filing cabinet.

I have met her. I interviewed her several times for a couple of different newspapers. But I don't really *know* her, except through her compelling book, a few long, good conversations, and a newsletter that comes to the house and reports on all things Jett Williams. She once let my young niece Chelsey, a huge Hank fan, hold Hank's hat, and I've always adored Cathy, aka Jett Williams, for that generous gesture.

Growing up in the same state at the same time, I figure we watched the same silly television shows, heard the same popular music, saw the same movies, sweated through the same humid summers, read *Know*

Alabama in fourth grade and called George Wallace governor. We both cheered from the same rung on the emotional development ladder as the Beatles landed on America's shores and man on the moon.

In a region that bronzed its baby shoes and Confederate heroes, we came of age. My story was typical. My childhood passed quietly with one family, my own, an ordinary, suburban Montgomery existence except for extended summer vacations spent in rural south Georgia. Cathy Deupree's story was unique, in the truest sense of that over-used word. Cathy was adopted by a financially comfortable Mobile couple, adults whose alcoholism and flawed love caused her not a few emotional struggles. And *that* was her second adoption, count 'em, two adoptions before she packed a book satchel and started school.

Yet we both had cowgirl suits and cherished them. She arrived in Mobile at age three with a little toy guitar. She loved to yodel, of all things, and to sing "Your Cheatin' Heart" standing on the dining room table at her grandmother's house. I had a pretend guitar and a coonskin cap and sang along to my father's Webb Pierce records: *I'm in the jailhouse now . . ."*

She went to Catholic schools, I went to public. After high school, Cathy headed for the University of Alabama in Tuscaloosa. I went up the road to the other state school, Auburn. The voice of Hank Williams was all around us all those growing-up years, same as the air we breathed, the red dirt beneath bare feet. We both heard it, loud and clear. Alabama had precious little iconic fodder about which to brag. Helen Keller, Bear Bryant, Hank Williams. They were the holy trinity of Alabama legends, and we worked with what we had. (Nobody in white public schools in the 1960s bothered to teach us us about native sons Nat King Cole or W. C. Handy or Jesse Owens or Willie Mays, though George Washington Carver and Booker T. Washington got cursory treatment.)

REALLY, OUR PATHS MIGHT never ever have crossed but for my profession, her story, my mother and her father. But this is confusing and I'm getting ahead of myself.

There was this strikingly glamorous couple in Monroeville, Alabama, of all places, casual friends of mine when I worked for the newspaper there. I admired both man and wife, separately and apart. They were social and political liberals, for one thing, an oddity in that ultra-conservative community. She looked like a young Elizabeth Taylor and worked for the welfare department. He was a progressive Unitarian minister and had dark curly hair and piercing eyes and was almost as beautiful as his wife. He opened doors for her and complimented her in sincere tones in front of others. They were perfect together, or so I thought.

He left her for another woman.

There are so few true storybook romances, especially marital ones. Time has taught this flinty-eyed reporter to expect the worst whenever people seem ostentatiously nuts about one another. And nothing seals a couple's fate like praising them as perfect, even if it's silent praise, muttered only in your own head.

So I was dubious when Hank Williams's so-called "lost daughter" told me over the telephone one day that she had divorced her husband and married her lawyer. By now Cathy was an aspiring country singer who in her third decade had given herself a new life, a new profession and a new name, her eighth one: Jett Williams.

Jett is the child of Hank and his sometimes-but-often-enough lover Bobbie Jett. Bobbie Jett was a Nashville secretary from a prosperous Tennessee family who caught the singer's eye near the end of his rocky marriage to Audrey. Before his death and his daughter's birth, Hank claimed the expected child as his own, made both physical and financial provisions for her, and left a contractual paper trail that should have settled the matter, forever and ever, amen. He even prearranged to have Cathy live with him when she turned three, or old enough to leave her grandmother's side. The contract outlining this arrangement has the *only* notarized signature of Hank's known to exist.

But everyone's lack of control beyond death is a given. In this case, legendary. As Jett succinctly puts it: "It's easy to beat a dead man and a baby."

People like neat stories, uncluttered with uneasy facts. That would explain why most Alabamians, even many who knew better, even little Cathy Deupree and I, liked the horrible 1964 movie about Hank called *Your Cheatin' Heart*, starring George Hamilton. Yes, that George Hamilton. I cried when I first saw it, so sad and melodramatic was the fictional story. Cathy did, too. Cathy and I had an excuse. We were only eleven.

In that trumped-up Hollywood version of his life, Hank was in most ways as clean-cut as a Salt Lake City Jaycee. When Hank dies in the movie, when his sins do him in, he is not divorced from Audrey, much less remarried to the voluptuous Louisiana looker Billie Jean Jones. For Hollywood purposes, he certainly is not the father of an illegitimate, oblivious daughter who, at the time of the movie's release, would have been a decade and two adoptions into the Alabama State Department of Pensions and Securities' secrets and system.

Nobody likes a messy ending.

WHEN JETT'S STORY SURFACED in the 1980s, it took most of us by complete surprise. Many in this world rife with pretenders and con artists were skeptical. Others downright disdainful. Who can blame them? Even Jerry Rivers, fiddler for the Drifting Cowboys and arguably one of Hank's best friends, at first couldn't believe Hank had a daughter. Later, like most of the world, he'd become convinced. He eventually would play behind Jett with the other remaining members of Hank's Drifting Cowboys band. But in the early 1980s, when Jett's existence first became widely known, Rivers told Pat and Don Grierson he didn't believe the story:

The only thing I know is what I read in the papers, all talking about Hank and "his longtime lover." Now you don't live with a guy, day and night, on the road traveling, more than his wife and children and everything, and not be aware of a "longtime lover." Now I knew a few thirty-minute lovers [of Hank's], but not longtime ones . . .

It wasn't just a court fight. Jett was giving a beloved, familiar story a new surprise ending.

Her long legal battle didn't begin in earnest till 1984, when she was thirty and met Washington lawyer Keith Adkinson. Cathy, as Jett was still known then, first learned of her possible parentage when she was twenty-one. Her adoptive parents, the Wayne Deuprees of Mobile, paid their daughter a birthday visit at the University of Alabama. Their visit had a second purpose. They had come to tell their Cathy she had been left $2,000 by Hank Williams's mother's estate. What? Why? Because Hank Williams might be her birth father, Louise Deupree said. The Deuprees were quick to add: There is no real proof. Her mother even advised Cathy to forget all about it.

Right.

I have tried to imagine being Cathy on that day. She certainly already knew she was adopted, even had fond if gauzy memories of her first foster family. But the rest of that sketchy news was a bolt from the blue. Or from heaven, if you are a Hank Williams fan.

Cathy didn't think she'd ever been to the city of Montgomery, for heaven's sake, much less lived there with Hank's mother for her first two years. Hank Williams her father? He wasn't even her first guess when Louise Deupree told her she might be the progeny of a famous Alabama singer. "Nat King Cole?" the funny Cathy guessed. She wasn't even a country music or Hank Williams fan exclusively; she wasn't the right generation for that.

"When I was in high school, I was into all kinds of music that was riding the air waves at the time," Jett recalls. "I . . . adored the Hank songs I heard, but I also adored the Motown Sound, the Beach Boys, the Mamas and the Papas and whatever else came out of the radio . . . Looking back, if four cars pulled up together with their radios on, we would all be singing, or trying to sing, the same song . . ."

But this. This was a shocker. What would you do? What would you think? It sounds as improbable as a fairy tale, and only the $2,000 check might have made this news seem something other than fantastic folderol. Besides, Cathy was a young woman finishing college and about to be married, embracing the conventional life that had sometimes eluded her in that topsy-turvy childhood. Now all of a sudden it was as if Louisa Mae Alcott had written *An Old Fashioned Girl* while on hallucinogens, making Cathy the innocent heroine.

She went to the Montgomery County courthouse and picked up the unexpected check. And that might have been the end of it. But Cathy couldn't just forget that beanstalk seed the Deuprees had planted in her blond head. She tried to find clues in newspaper archives and in books about her famous dad. She became a kind of Nancy Drew, girl sleuth, trying to unlock the Secret in the Troubadour's Trunk. Cathy made inquiries, met with her half-siblings on her mother's side and slowly, over a decade, decided that something in her past was a state secret. Literally. Most of the court records had been sealed, and Cathy ran up against more walls than an unlucky NASCAR driver.

It was a slow go. After all, she was married. She worked in a Montgomery suburb for the recreation department. She had a real, workaday existence that had little to do with country legends. Despite all that, she eventually learned enough to convince herself. To believe in her heart of hearts she was Hank's daughter. Too many people seemed to *expect* her questions. When, for instance, she phoned Charles Carr, who as a teenager was hired to drive Hank to Ohio and was with him when he died, she found Carr knew all about her and wasn't the least surprised to receive her call from the blue. Ironies abounded. It seemed, at times, like almost everyone in Montgomery knew her story, all the characters and plot twists, but nobody was willing to share it with her, the hapless heroine. As one lawyer making money off her ignorance put it in a letter to another lawyer: *"We've got her buried; she'll never find out."*

Even after partnering with the aggressive Adkinson, her "knight in a three-piece suit," as Jett describes her husband, it would be an uphill struggle. It would take nine years and complicated court fights to satisfy the world that she is Hank's daughter and, that settled, deserving of her share of his valuable estate.

Through the first two decades of Jett's life it had been almost too easy to dupe the dead man and the baby. Lawyers working for Audrey and Hank Jr. and Acuff-Rose Publishers, among others, were loathe to divide royalties. In concert with a whole cast of obliging Alabama bureaucrats, the system successfully cheated Jett out of her rightful inheritance. It was, in a word, *fraud*, a successful fraud.

SHE MIGHT NEVER HAVE even known but for that check. Follow the money, as they say. Hank's mother, Jett's grandmother, the formidable Lillian Stone (Lilly, also Lillie), had taken Cathy in when she was born five days after Hank's death in 1953. Not only did Lillian embrace Hank's baby, as she had promised Hank she would, she jumped through considerable hoops to adopt her granddaughter. That couldn't have been easy in the Deep South for a multiple divorcee with a heart condition. Everything about this story might have been dramatically different if Lillian Stone had not died at the middle age of fifty-seven within weeks of the adoption.

When Lillian died, the toddler Cathy Yvonne Stone was once again without a family and was turned over to the Montgomery County Department of Public Welfare and a licensed boarding home. Babies are resilient. She drew a good foster family. But she wouldn't stay at that loving home long, either.

Adopted again just before school age by the Deuprees of Mobile, Cathy turned out well, despite the rough beginning and alcoholic parents. She graduated from Alabama and married her college sweetheart, Michael Mayer, in 1975.

"I think we married for the reason many kids marry right out of college," Jett would write in her 1990 memoir, *Ain't Nothing as Sweet as My Baby*. "We didn't know what else to do."

But you don't drop the "H" bomb into a smart young woman's head and expect her to forget all about it. Not a determined and inquisitive woman like Cathy.

A serious Hank junkie, I followed her case from the beginning. Before she knew how to fight or if she would, really. And, every now and again, I'd telephone to see how the war was going. One day she had news that didn't directly concern her legal fight.

She was crazy in love, she said to me, and living on a houseboat on the Potomac in Washington, D.C. She had married that handsome lawyer she'd engaged two years earlier to help her prove she was Hank's daughter.

Don't get me wrong. I didn't blame her. Keith Adkinson is not only nice-looking—Kris Kristofferson with a tad more Indian blood—but a tough, flamboyant, give-'em-hell advocate who would, in time, not only secure Jett's rightful part of the ever-growing Hank fortune, but also put her on the path to an obvious music career. But, at first, it all seemed so sudden and unlikely, I had to wonder and worry. There was too much unbridled admiration, I thought. I was a true newspaper cynic. One year, much later, Keith gave Jett two minks, a chinchilla coat, and a red Jeep, all in the space of a few weeks.

Jett was pinching herself for a while, as well, she admits, but not with any doubts about Keith. No doubts there. She was questioning if everything so wonderful and happening so fast was real.

"If I made my life up, reality would trump fiction. My husband . . . and I often reflect on 'Has all of this really happened?'"

Keith and Jett have now been married twenty-five years and live on the seven hundred-acre farm in a Tennessee Eden. They know all of their neighbors in a community "as close as you can get to how the world was in my childhood," Jett says, populated by ordinary people who are there when you need them but respect your privacy otherwise. Jett says they have "dug in," even establishing a family cemetery on the place. Keith's mother and aunt are buried there. They have embraced Jett's fate and find fun and satisfaction in promoting all things Hank. They do everything together and have spent precious few nights apart. The first time they parted was in East Germany, of all places, when Keith, involved in a federal court case at the time, was served with a subpoena and forced to fly home.

I think this one is going to last.

BUT I'LL ADMIT, AT first, I fretted a lot about Jett, or Cathy, as I still thought of her then. She has a vulnerability that is both winning and worrisome. There's been so much written and said about how she looks like Hank. And it's true. You can see, and hear, Hank in Jett Williams. She has his sad, sad eyes and thin, serious lips. But she also has her mother's comely features and fair skin. Always a tomboy, Jett's beauty is the natural kind, with long flaxen hair, straight as a Delta highway, framing an honest face. What's most endearing is her disposition, sweet, with a penumbra of glowing honesty. If you were sitting beside her in a bus station, you'd feel fine asking her to watch your suitcase while you bought your ticket.

It wasn't fair that someone so guileless had to start her life as a country singer, her life as Hank's daughter, by going up against the hoary Nashville establishment. Not to mention by necessarily shattering the false images of Audrey and Hank that people who don't know any better, and some who did, were clinging to. After all, if Audrey could pass herself off as Hank's widow—on the silver screen, no less—there had to be some who were perfectly willing to dismiss Jett's claims as fiction, though they were indisputably fact. In characteristic fashion, Jett today makes light of the struggle to win *hearts* as well as court cases.

"Every aspiring country artist should make their debut in Nashville by suing Hank Wiliams Jr., Roy Acuff, Wesley Rose, Opryland, Acuff-Rose Music, and a host of others," Jett says. "But that's what happened. It was a David versus Goliath deal from the get-go . . ."

And it was. Classic and almost biblical. Right makes might. That kind of thing. Turns out, the meek *shall* inherit the earth, or at least Hank's hat. I heard about Jett's story early on, about the time she finally had decided to pursue her unique heritage in the courts, if necessary. And the *way* I first heard about Hank Williams's daughter still astounds me.

You learn to expect precious little from family and friends in terms of column ideas. I'm speaking with thirty-five years' worth of experience. Your best ideas come from strangers, from readers, occasionally from editors, but almost never from family and friends. Except, of course, the inadvertent inspiration you get from bizarre familial behavior and reunions.

Your sister might discover the cure for cancer, but she'd forget to tell you. Your father might meet Gandhi and not mention it. That's just the way it goes. It's not an intentional thing, but a real aggravation nevertheless.

Mother, especially, has always been sweetly oblivious to what I do for a living. She hates that I write, but loves me having written. So, I didn't pay all that much attention when one day in 1981 she phoned out of the blue and said, "I've got a good story for you."

"Uh-huh."

Then she allowed as to how she first heard this scoop at the beauty shop in Pine Level, Alabama, the small community, several shades shy of a town, where my folks have lived since the late 1970s. There are, interestingly enough, two Pine Levels. One just North of Montgomery, and another, the one I know so well, about seventeen miles south of Montgomery. Pine Level South consists of a water tank, a library in a trailer, a few churches of all the usual flavors, and a western wear store everyone calls "the Blue Jean Mall." And, of course, a beauty shop.

When Mother mentioned that her source for this scoop was the beauty shop, I couldn't help but think of the wonderful Eudora Welty short story "Petrified Man," in which vicious women gossips torture one another with good stories and bad permanents. Beauty shop gossip, entertaining as it is, doesn't always qualify as reliable.

Mother continued. I listened. I had to admit it was an amazing tale, preposterous but intriguing. It was so interesting I couldn't believe my mother had thought to tell me.

Hank Williams has an illegitimate daughter, Mother matter-of-factly said. What's more, this mystery daughter once was a foster child of Pine Level neighbors, Henry and Ilda Mae Cook. Her name is Cathy Deupree Mayer, Mother continued, and—oh, yes—she now lives and works in Montgomery.

I don't remember how I found the phone number. I probably called the Cooks, whom I knew through my parents. Their son, Jimmy, was a friend of Daddy's.

Soon enough I reached Cathy Mayer, introduced myself and told her what I'd heard. From my mother. Who heard it at a beauty shop. I spoke apologetically at first because the story seemed so far-fetched. How in heaven's name would my mother be among the first to know something like this? If it were true, wouldn't this be big news? Wouldn't it be all over the television and on front pages everywhere? I had never been all that great at getting to big news first. My specialty was moving in to make sense of things once the press conference dust settled.

It was true, Cathy said. She had reason to believe Hank Williams might have been her father. She had no hard proof. She might or might not hire a lawyer. Cathy and I had a nice, if brief conversation. She had a polite, Southern accent, and was modest to a fault. I'll never forget what she said just before we said goodbye.

"Do you think anybody would really be interested in all that?"

I answered with an emphatic, "Yes!"

"If I thought Hank Williams might be my father, I'd spend the rest of my life trying to prove it," I said before eliciting a promise that she would "give" me the story first if ever she did "try to prove it." We ended the conversation. We didn't speak again for a while, though every now and again I'd phone her and ask to write a column about her quest.

I DIDN'T GET TO "break" the story that kicked off the nine years of litigation. That was disappointing to me, but understandable. When Keith orchestrated the 1985 press conference, a Rubicon that would "introduce" Hank's daughter to the world, he naturally went for an Alabama setting and a national audience. Cathy wasn't at the press conference, and neither was I. I was angry when I heard about it, but anger will get you nowhere in the story-breaking business. At the time I was working for the Memphis newspaper, the *Commercial Appeal*, pretty far off Keith's radar. Not the heart of Hank country.

Soon enough, I got back on that pony, even visiting the newlyweds once on their antique, seventy-two-foot Washington-based yacht, the *JettStream*. It now floats on the Cumberland River in Nashville, but at the time I saw it was at a marina on the Potomac. That spectacular ship would have been reason enough to hook up with Adkinson. Originally called the *Queen of the Potomac*, the yacht had been newly renovated and re-christened. It had been Edward G. Robinson's getaway vessel in the movie *Key Largo*, what Keith Adkinson wryly calls his yacht's "fifteen frames of fame."

I would write a column about that D.C. visit and several others about the couple and their amazing life through the years. Cathy, even in my stubborn mind, had become Jett and, I'll admit, better and better copy.

In case you are wondering—and heaven knows I was—the Pine Level gossip Mother had heard four years before had resulted from Cathy's presence at the Cooks' fiftieth wedding anniversary. For Cathy, they had been Mama and Daddy Cook, country folks with kind faces and big hearts who provided a good home and love for a year right after her grandmother died. The anniversary party was the first time Cathy had seen the Cooks since she was three years old, and she was nervous about the reunion.

She drove her Triumph Spitfire south from Montgomery down U.S. 231, commonly called the Troy Highway. She would have passed cattle ranches and fireworks stands and service stations galore, the same route I take to see my folks. She drove her little sports car up to the Pine Level Methodist church where the celebration was being held, and Jimmy Cook, who had been a teenager the year Cathy stayed with the family, was sitting on the steps waiting for her. He even took from his billfold a photograph of her he'd been carrying around all this years, hoping someday to reconnect with his "sister."

"When we met, I knew I was in for a warm and loving experience; there wasn't going to be any rejection here," Jett says.

She was born Antha Belle Jett, that name being Bobbie Jett's only gift to her daughter. That moniker wouldn't last long. Lillian Stone changed the baby's name to Cathy Yvone Stone, misspelling the reference to the Yvvone—"sweetest one"—mentioned in Hank's song "Jambalaya." After her year with the Cooks, Cathy went to live with the Deuprees in Mobile. But there was no official adoption, not right away. The Deuprees knew enough to remain cautious. Hank's sister, Irene, had sued the baby to prevent her from inheriting from Lillian. The state had advised the Deuprees not to adopt until the litigation was over. She would be school age before becoming Cathy Louise Deupree.

When she married after college, she became Cathy Mayer. Finally, embracing her fate and, with Keith's help, beginning a singing career, she renamed herself Jett Williams. The catchy name that's been in lights has stuck, but I can't help but wonder what name she uses for herself in private thoughts.

Changing her name was easy. *Claiming* the "Williams" part, giving it heft, was tough. Her fateful return to Pine Level was years before she would proven her identity. But somehow, just knowing she'd been loved by her first foster family gave her the courage she needed to continue her search.

"Daddy Cook rode with me in the small sports car and pointed out all the things of interest to him, and what he thought would be of interest to me. It all felt vaguely familiar in a positive way, but when we got to the home I knew something wasn't right. That's because the home I lived in with them had burned, and what I was looking at was a new home.

"The long and short of it is, they made me feel so special, and that was something I was not used to . . . The family that took me next [after the Cooks] had a somewhat different attitude. I am just thankful to have been reunited with a real family that actually cared for me, even if I was just a foster child. The Cooks were truly good people, and they were certainly kind to a confused two-year-old back in 1955 or 1956."

Again, that matter of first memories comes into play. Jett's first memories probably would not have been from the short time she spent with Lillian at her legendary Montgomery boarding house. It seems more reasonable that Jett's first recall would be from around the age of three, when she was embraced warmly by the Cooks, who, yes, had heard rumors she was Hank's daughter. Montgomery was a small town in those days, and births out of wedlock, especially when one of the parents was a legend, generated plenty of gossip.

If a reunion with the Cooks gave her courage to fight, meeting Keith Adkinson gave her a way. A mutual friend told her about the lawyer, and she phoned him when he visited Mobile on another case. Not only did he listen to her legal woes, he listened to her sing. And with that impromptu concert Jett's life took a dramatic turn. Keith, quite literally, was on the case.

"During the dark days when I was being pilloried by 'the bad guys' and thought my name was 'Illegitimate' or 'Alleged' it got me down," she says. "I never let them know it, but I would collapse in Keith's arms and cry after being mauled by eighteen lawyers who made me feel like a rape victim.

"I just didn't get it. How could they be so mean? I hadn't done anything to them, they had done it to me . . ."

In 1987, in a forty-four-page document, the Alabama Supreme Court agreed. The court made the pronouncement that mattered most to Jett. The justices said that ". . . unlike many cases in which the alleged father denies paternity and wishes to have nothing to do with the child, this is a case in which the father not only wished to accept responsibility for the child, but convinced the mother to give the child up, so that it might live with him and be reared by him."

SHE WAS HANK WILLIAMS daughter, and he had wanted her. Amen. Hallelujah. Now back to court to get a daughter's share.

The most appealing thing about Jett—aside from her voice, which is truly good enough to get attention even if her name were *Williamson* instead of *Williams*—is how she refuses to cry over spilt milk. She says things like: "Since I met Keith, I have been blessed with a million 'once in a lifetimes' and we ain't done yet. If I'm not performing or promoting The Great One [her phrase for Hank], we are fishing; if we aren't fishing, we're hunting; if we aren't doing either, we're smelling the flowers . . ."

Until she died, the wanna-be widow Audrey had seen to it that her son Hank Jr. took full advantage of his famous name and legacy. As Paul Hemphill writes in *Lovesick Blues*,

> Hank, Jr., was cursed by the name from the start, and his mother made things worse even while the boy was still tooling around Nashville in the convertible in which his father had died. Audrey was calling every shot in the poor kid's life, forcing Hank's music on him—she booked him for his debut at fourteen in the auditorium at Canton, Ohio, on the anniversary of the concert Hank never made—and for a while he put on an eerie act . . .

But Hank Jr. wasn't the only kid who rode around in his daddy's blue Cadillac. Move over, Bocephus. Grandma Lillian gave her precious little granddaughter/adopted daughter Cathy rides around town in the Cadillac as well. Jett is human enough to wonder occasionally how her life might have been what she calls "cataclysmically different" had Lillian Stone lived a while longer.

"When we got started on our odyssey, Keith said, 'How different would your life have been if someone had put you in a little cowgirl suit at age four and patted you on the butt as you walked on stage at the *Grand Ole Opry*?' We'll never know, but one thing for sure, it may have been a rocky start, but I'm just delighted how it turned out."

She doesn't dwell on what-ifs.

There's too much else to do. Not only has the marriage lasted, Jett's singing career has as well. Given the advantage of the name, it was easy to get bookings the first time around. Repeat performances are something else. She gets *invited back,* and that's because Jett is a good entertainer, a trouper, if you will. Hank's blood is inside her. Four of her songs are featured on a soundtrack for a new Harry Thompson movie about a famous country singer's last ride.

These surreal *moments,* those "once in a lifetimes," keep on happening. Like the time she was invited to sing on the *Louisiana Hayride* and had planned to perform "I Saw the Light." Willie Nelson was on the show the same night, and he had the same plan.

"I thought, *That's fine. Willie should sing it."* But Willie, being Willie, sent word to her dressing room that he would love it if Jett would join him in performing that famous number. She did. And while she was standing on that legendary Shreveport stage next to Willie Nelson—*Willie Nelson!*—singing her father's song, Willie leans over to her and says, "Jett, your daddy was my hero."

That's the kind of moment that makes up for a lot of courtroom tedium.

And it hasn't ended. She was nominated for a Grammy after producing *The Unreleased Recordings of Hank Williams*, a trove of Hank covers a fan might have dreamed up. The Beatles beat her out, which is not a bad way to lose if you must. In 2010 she picked up Hank's Pulitzer Prize at Columbia University, which she calls the highest high of them all.

"As I sing my daddy's songs or play them on my radio show, I cannot help but reflect upon their penetration of one's very bone marrow. Especially mine," she says.

"Knowing what I know now—being named for the 'Yvonne' in 'Jambalaya'; being born to my mother singing 'I Can't Help It If I'm Still in Love with You' in the delivery room . . .; being in the womb and a few months away from birth when my mom and dad were at Lake Martin one fateful weekend in August 1952, when he wrote 'Kaw-liga' and 'Your Cheatin' Heart'—Lordy, I feel like the muses are upon me, and I cherish it."

Of all those on earth who think Hank hung the moon, Jett thinks he hung it highest. When she talks about him, her face, still unlined at fifty-eight, looks awestruck, the way my niece looked the first time she heard a Hank song. Jett's favorite song, "I'm So Lonesome I Could Cry," is, she says, "a work of art. It's not necessarily a love song. He could be missing a friend, a child, a pet. He never tells you who it is." And that brilliant stroke—a *lack* of particulars—gives the song universality, meaning, that few have.

At times I live vicariously through Jett Williams's happy ending, proof that sometimes life sorts itself out and good guys and sweet girls come out on top. That's not an ending you write a lot in the newspaper business. Jett's story, for my money, is right up there with Kate Middleton's or Lana Turner's fairy tales. One day you're a commoner, a nobody sipping a soda at the Top Hat Café. (It wasn't Schwab's, by the way.) The next day, you're a princess, a movie star, Hank Williams's daughter.

And the best part is that despite the money, the new name, the singing career, Jett Williams remains the same sweet soul I first talked to when both of us were young. She tools around the Tennessee countryside in the same red Chevrolet pickup she bought twenty-five years ago. She plants her own corn in a field near the house. Her baby shoes sold on eBay, but some nice stranger mailed them to her and Jett had them framed.

Amongst all the photographs, posters, records, and funky memorabilia that soon mount up if you are Hank's blood kin is a pretty china tea set, German-made. A venerable Montgomery pawn shop sent it to Jett. Grandma Lillian had put the $14.95 set of dishes on layaway at the pawn shop and died before she could finish paying. She owed $1.

Jett Williams accepted the gift but paid the balance.

CHAPTER FOUR

*"All one has to do is hit the right keys at the right time
and the instrument plays itself."*

— JOHANN SEBASTIAN BACH

Hazel Etheridge couldn't have stood more than five feet tall. She wore compensating tall heels and stylish pedal pushers and bright nail polish, and she was as vivacious as a game show host. She taught me piano. Or tried.

Once a week for several years, I'd walk the dozen suburban blocks from our house to hers where she gave private lessons in a den she called her "studio." She was perpetually sweet and forgiving, full of both life and patience, and as a result I loved her. She loved me, too, which probably wasn't the best overall arrangement to nudge music from my reluctant soul.

Mrs. Etheridge had excess energy, and could do more than one thing at once. Often, while I banged out a tortured version of whatever song I was supposed to have mastered during the week, she would cook supper in the next room. I'd butcher a measure, and she'd peek around the corner of the den, smiling big, holding her cooking spoon high in a classic conductor's pose. She'd then act as a human metronome to show me how the music should have been paced.

"Da-da-de-dah-dah, da-de-da-de-dah," she'd sing, emphasizing the down beat. And I, no prodigy to say the least, would plow through "Country Gardens" again and again.

She wasn't my first piano teacher, or my last, but she was my favorite by far. Daddy wanted us to share his passion, and so we started taking lessons early. Probably too early. I'm pretty sure he never got his money's worth.

JoAnne, three years older than I, began piano lessons first. We were living in Pensacola, Florida, and Mother somehow heard about a German man nearby who owned a music store and taught piano lessons after closing time. Mother, JoAnne and I paid him a call. I remember our trio tromping up a steep set of outside stairs to his apartment above the store for JoAnne to audition. I was fascinated by the stern-looking man's heavy accent, and his thick bifocals. He looked more a rocket scientist than a pianist.

After our younger sister Sheila was born and Mother was homebound, the accommodating German came to our house and, eventually, taught me as well. JoAnne always had more talent and discipline and was interested in music theory. She actually practiced. I, on the other hand, had what our parents optimistically called "an ear for music." I couldn't easily read or play the notes from the page, but I didn't care. If I heard a song, generally I could rush to the piano and recreate it in the key of C; that is to say, no accidentals.

When I used one plump finger to pick out "Hang Down Your Head Tom Dooley" on JoAnne's fine new spinet, Daddy decided I was the female Liberace and merited lessons as well. I took only a few weeks of lessons before the obligatory recital was scheduled. Recitals, as anyone who was ever within three miles of one knows, are torture, for everyone, but the fear they induce forges notes into your head forever. Fifty years have passed, and I still can play "by heart" every recital piece I ever mastered, including the first one.

The trick was to perfect by memory your recital piece before the nerve-rattling event. Because I'd only just begun and had worked on songs from beginner songbooks with not only words but illustrations—"Putt, putt, putt, putt, putt, putt. Goes the little speedboat"—it must have been hard to come up with a recital assignment for me. The German did. I dutifully worked at remembering a short song called "The Cowgirl," a simple but lively, wordless composition that I loved playing.

The night came, and I was ready. Mother had pin-curled my hair and ironed my Easter dress. JoAnne and I got into trouble before we ever left the house for asking too many times if it was time to go. Eager beavers with Shirley Temple heads. My grandmother was in town, coincidentally I hope, and able to attend.

Recitals then, and probably now, were always arranged so that beginners performed first, then mid-level students, the amateur hour, or hours, gradually working its way toward the veterans, those who actually knew their asses from a treble clef. If ever I run a piano recital, which is about as likely as my running the country, I'd intersperse the "comic relief" throughout the program. That way you'd get an amusing meltdown or two between the Brahms and the Chopin.

When it came my time to perform, second on the program, I ran to the piano, threw myself at the keyboard and played the piece without missing a note—but also without nuance, proper pauses, or any variation in volume—finishing in record time my flat-out, scalding rendition. Then this cowgirl galloped back to her seat. All I really remember is that the audience laughed. My father sighed. My grandmother said I was brilliant.

Not long after my first recital, my father was transferred by the Winn-Dixie grocery chain to Montgomery, Alabama, a regional headquarters, cutting short my humiliation and lessons with the German. My vacation from the piano was short, however. Soon after the big move Mother enrolled us in piano lessons with Mrs. Etheridge. And when that wound down, Mrs. Etheridge told Mother how you could pay for private lessons at Huntingdon College, Montgomery's respected liberal arts school. That sounded just dandy, Huntingdon being an oasis of culture in Montgomery's Old Cloverdale community. We had been to ballets on the lawn there, and once I'd picked up a dozen white rats from a biology classroom for my science experiment. JoAnne, more advanced, was to be taught by a regular piano instructor at the college, and I by one of her students.

Miss Bonita, my Huntingdon teacher, was a serious young lady who wore all brown: pleated wool skirts, sweaters, and penny loafers. Her hair was brown. Her knee socks were brown. The room seemed brown. She had a real thing for Bach. I hated Bach. To me a Bach sonata sounded like you were making the song up as you went along, a jazzed-up scale with no harmony or chorus, a cat on the keyboard stepping gingerly. It was, well, *beige* music, certainly in the brown family.

I desperately wanted to play the *good* stuff, songs with rich melodies and interesting words. I wanted to play Hank Williams. And often I did, picking out "My Bucket's Got a Hole in It" or "Cool Water" when I was supposed to be practicing Bach. I quickly learned you could play any Hank song in the key of C. Mother was busy with two younger children by now, so as long as I beat out something, anything, during practice time, nobody noticed. I would sit for the obligatory hour picking out Hank Williams with one finger. If Mother walked by, I'd quickly place both hands on the keyboard, curving them just so the way I'd been taught, as if a small red rubber ball was beneath them.

As it happened, my Grandma Lucille played like I aspired to, and she'd only had two or three free lessons from a country neighbor woman. No dawdling about for years on theory and prep for her. Lucille used a method called "chording," with the right hand playing the melody and the left matching with the correct major chord, broken down into something that had a syncopated accent. She bought herself an old upright and put it in the little living room she'd created by closing in half the front porch. She'd play and sing and have a wonderful time by herself.

Her style on the old upright made every song sound ragtime, even the Baptist hymns, and the bric-a-brac atop the piano rattled as she banged the hell out of "Softly and Tenderly." There was nothing brown about the way *she* played. If assigned a color, it would have been red. And Bach himself would have been impressed had he been transported to that time and place, a dirt road in south Georgia where all tunes were loud and lively.

I didn't think about it much as a child, but I realize now it's admirable that my grandmother attempted to learn to play so relatively late in her life. She was in her seventies before she even had time to consider taking piano lessons. I think perhaps it was the *Lawrence Welk Show* that convinced her to try. There is some irony there, because she could turn shrill in a heartbeat whenever the show's flamboyant pianist, Joanne Castle, took the stage: "Look at her, bouncing around on that stool like she's got ants in her pants." Lucille thought Joanne lacked gravitas and was a man-hungry showboat. I'm paraphrasing, but you get the picture.

By now Lucille had sold the hogs and given up on big gardens and had winnowed her workload down to cooking three huge meals a day. Nothing to it, a baby could do it. That gave her time to master piano, and she did. If Jerry Lee Lewis had been held in the starting gate for seven decades, he might have sounded like Lucille—passionately urgent.

Once when I visited, Grandma Lucille taught me "Redwing," and I substituted it for Bach at every opportunity. On that one song, I almost sounded good. I could also play by ear hymns from the Broadman Hymnal, Stephen Foster songs about happy darkies, and anything I heard on the AM radio, including, of course, Hank Williams. I mastered the melody of "Hey, Good Lookin'" and played it over and over with one hand. On the "brand new recipe" part I pushed down hard on the piano's pedal, figuring that's where Hank would want the emphasis to be.

The Huntingdon lessons didn't last long. The college was all the way across town, and, in those days, crossing town was akin to swimming the English Channel. We just didn't do it much. And I missed Mrs. Etheridge—who lived closer and charged less. I stopped practicing altogether, a strike not heard 'round the world. With Mrs. Etheridge, at least, I had tried to practice because she was the type of adult you wanted to please. There weren't many. She propped me up in duets, making what little I knew sound good by taking over the harder, I thought, bass parts. I loved playing duets, either with JoAnne or Mrs. Etheridge, but I still couldn't sight-read if you threw in a few sharps and flats.

It was becoming clear I had more interest in spinning records than practicing scales. I begged to stop taking piano lessons and take up the guitar. The guitar was where it was at in the 1960s. Peter, Paul, and Mary blew in the wind; they weren't anchored to a piano stool.

"You can quit," Daddy said. "But you have to take either steel guitar or accordion."

How he settled so quickly on *one* of those two instruments is no mystery.

The steel guitar was the signature instrument in all "real" country, still is. That familiar twang lets you know that something real is about to happen. Drums send the opposite signal. The Drifting Cowboys' steel guitar player, the late Don Helms, was one of the nation's best steel guitarists, helping to create the distinctive sound that was Hank Williams. A steel guitar cries so you don't have to.

The accordion, I'm not so sure about. I have no idea how Daddy came up with that choice; he simply liked the sound. Many country bands, including Hank's, had used accordionists in the 1930s and '40s. Pee Wee Moultrie played accordion for Hank from 1938 to 1940 when both musicians were only teenagers. Pee Wee's accordion was showcased on such songs as "Alexander's Ragtime Band" and "Fan It." There were, in fact, as many as sixty active accordionists in the 1930s, playing with country bands broadcast most notably by Chicago's *National Barn Dance* radio show. It's said Gene Autry chose his sidekick Smiley Burnette because he played a mean accordion.

The trend didn't last. I don't know why. The Sears catalog described the instrument as an "orchestra in a box." Seems as volume would be reason enough to keep the squeeze box behind you. Few singers did, an exception being Texas swing and zydeco.

Only in recent years has the accordion again been incorporated into mainstream country music. Lucinda Williams, one of my favorite progressive country singers, uses accordion accents in many of her Louisiana-based songs and nothing, but nothing, sounds better.

Daddy somehow instinctively knew an accordion would suit me. He threw in steel guitar so I'd have a choice and feel I had a vote. At first I wasn't thrilled by the prospect of learning either instrument.

Just my luck that there would be an accomplished accordionist and instructor in the neighborhood. By now I was twelve, a six-year veteran of taking piano lessons that didn't take, and totally unaware that already Lawrence Welk had done to the accordion what television's *Hee Haw* would soon do to country music—he had rendered it a joke.

My teacher was a woman, a kind, handsome, and dignified person whose husband taught guitar. They sat all day in side-by-side sound-proofed rooms teaching their respective instruments. They might as well have been a million miles apart.

Because I already could play the keyboard, my instructor loaned me a piano accordion and a thick book full of popular songs—*and with words!*—on my second or third visit. It was a great departure from the piano music I'd been playing. The songbook included popular favorites like "Autumn Leaves," "Give My Regards to Broadway," and "Beer Barrel Polka." There was even an easy-to-play version of "Cold, Cold Heart."

This was more like it.

I took to the accordion, willingly locking myself for daily practice in the half bath of our bath-and-a-half house, enjoying the acoustics that the tile walls provided. My parents soon invested in a woman's-size, glittering blue Italian model called a Scandali just for me. It had the shine of a new bass boat and more bells and whistles than I could have dreamed possible. You could push one button to have your music sound like a clarinet, another to make it mimic a bass. It was the instrument for me, what with the right hand playing the melody, and the left blindly locating the pre-set chord buttons. I could play the accordion the same way Grandma Lucille had played the piano. It came quite naturally.

I've read that you can trace the accordion's roots back to the birth of music itself, an instrument called the cheng that used a free vibrating reed. The cheng supposedly was invented during the reign of the legendary "Yellow Emperor," Huang Ti, around 3000 B.C. His other achievements included the invention of boats, money, and religious sacrifice. Some might argue he should have stopped with religious sacrifice.

The first piano accordion dates to 1863 in Vienna. Performers considered it a liberation from walls of pipes. And I understood that mobility thing, too. All of a sudden I had a movable piano that I could take to the patio for a practice session, or to school for show and tell, or on a road trip to torture my relatives. I once played it in a cow pasture on a cookout with my cousin Marilyn Jo. I thought I was destined for musical greatness and almost wore the Scandali out playing Sunday concerts for my father, who I am sure sacrificed to buy the thing.

Then I started junior high school. Junior high schools are the cruelest places on earth. I'd just as soon drop off a child I loved at Mississippi's Parchman Prison farm as leave them to be tortured and ridiculed by a group of pre-pubescent thugs. Things would have been fine, no peers the wiser, had I not succumbed to some base need to show off. I deserved my fate. I was good at the accordion and knew it. So I entered a local talent show, winning second place and a red ribbon and the attention of a boy who otherwise wouldn't have known I was alive. Zane Smith, a tall, lanky fellow with few social skills, spent the rest of his junior high career following me down hallways making a squeezing motion with his arms and a honking noise with his big mouth.

I put the accordion away and quit lessons. Even my strict parents, whose will was law, couldn't force me to continue. I just would not do it. I never talked back, but I was capable of virtuoso pouts that would have reversed a papal edict.

My defeated father eventually bought me a guitar one Christmas, and I learned a few chords on my own and sang mostly the folk tunes so popular then. Where *had* all those damn flowers gone? I wasn't any good at the guitar, a fact that pains me still. I fretted over frets until the necessary calluses formed and my sisters ran for cover. But I never got any better, whatsoever.

It would be years before I found the self-confidence to get the accordion back out of its case and practice. Even then, after I began enjoying the music again, I had to know someone really well before I told them I could play the accordion.

I've forgotten most of the songs I knew back then. I still can play a few things by ear, mostly Hank Williams songs that sound pretty good in the key of C with the bass button pushed down. They sound mournful, the way they should.

In the name of duty while working for the Atlanta newspaper, I got to have dinner with Myron Floren, the showman with the perpetual smile who played accordion for Lawrence Welk for thirty years. The year was 1996. I wish I had met him earlier.

Floren said accordion jokes didn't bother him in the least, "as long as I'm playing 150 concerts a year." The accordion had been his ticket to a good life.

His folks were farmers with seven children in Webster, South Dakota. At age seven, Myron ordered a $19.95 buttonbox from Sears, Roebuck and Co. That was a lot of money, he explained, what with corn bringing only two cents a bushel at the time.

There were no music lessons in Webster, so little Myron taught himself, practicing before school and after chores. His father got into local politics and moved his family to town when Myron was sixteen. That's when he bought his first piano accordion, which he used later for teaching and working his way through college.

By the time Welk "discovered" Floren in 1950, he was a seasoned performer. He got twenty dollars a month for *The Melody Man* show on the Mutual Broadcasting Radio Network. And he worked for the USO in Europe in 1944, sometimes playing close enough to the front lines to hear the fighting. The USO wanted Myron to travel on to the Pacific, but he begged off to go home and marry Berdyne Koerner, his former accordion pupil. The USO plane he would have been on went down in New Guinea.

"I've had that kind of luck all my life," he told me. I guess that's why he can laugh so easily at accordion jokes.

A childhood case of rheumatic fever made him ineligible for active duty. His wedding plans kept him off a doomed airplane. And celebrating his wife's birthday by going to a Lawrence Welk performance launched his long television career.

Welk had heard Floren play at a fair. When he saw him in the audience, the bandleader invited Myron to join his orchestra for a song. Later that same night, Welk offered him a job. Accordion history was made.

In the 1960s, when I took up the accordion, the show became so unhip that the network wanted to cancel it. "They forgot that a lot of people live west of the Hudson River," Myron said. He, for one, never worried about TV trends or the show's square image. He just works an accordion joke or two into his own act, plays "How Great Thou Art" one more time, and otherwise goes on about his business.

Same as Myron, Hank Williams certainly never worried about whether he was hip or not. He resisted the occasional Fred Rose suggestion that he de-countrify his pronunciation of song lyrics. Hank instinctively knew that "crick" sounded better than "creek" to his brand of listeners, and that drinkin' and cheatin' songs didn't require that "g" on the end of the signature words. Drinkin' and cheatin' were sins of omission—the "g" was what you omitted.

If only I'd been as self-assured as Hank about my music, I might be the accordionist on Lucinda's *Car Wheels on a Gravel Road* album. I might have gone somewhere Zane Smith couldn't possibly follow. But, no, I lacked Hank's vision and backbone.

Hank approached his music the way Vincent Van Gogh approached a canvas. The artist attacked a painting with such intensity he sometimes tore the canvas. "How preposterous it is," he wrote, "to make oneself dependent on the opinion of others in what one does."

Hank Williams worked the same way. Passionately confident in his area of expertise.

I have read and subscribe to the theory that any writer worth her salt needs to take a few music lessons and some sailing lessons before attempting to write. A writer, goes the argument, needs to know the poetry and the lilting language of both pursuits, those phrases that sound like what they are: crescendo and listing, for examples. You call on the language of music and the sea at every turn to make prose pretty. They become the memorable phrases, the ones with salt and sea spray and—shall I say it?—rhythm.

Daddy saw to my music lessons, bless his heart. Jimmy tried in vain to teach me about sailing. So maybe all along, instead of preparing to be a concert pianist or an accordionist in Lucinda's hot band, maybe while stuttering through "Beer Barrel Polka" in that half-bath with its door closed, I simply was preparing to write.

"We could tell that he was destined for an early depar-
ture. Drugs and women. Sometimes great songs are
written this way. It's almost as if he had the drugs and
women to thank for the songs . . . Yet, it's very sad . . ."

— CHET ATKINS

CHAPTER FIVE

There is a perpetual nervousness about Hélène Boudreaux that can be explained by any number of things in her past life—an indifferent mother, abject poverty, beatings by a cruel husband, bad bargains with that Devil nicknamed "Necessity." Even today, in mellow maturity, when her life has taken a spin into a much calmer and healthier universe, Helen (as her name is spelled in English) often seems anxious.

One day when I visit her she's lost her rosary, and Helen is as fretful as a motherless pup. Her faith is important to her, and this tangible symbol gives constant comfort. She rocks back and forth, but in a straight chair, jumping up every now and again to check and see if she put the rosary in the bathroom, by the bed, over the kitchen sink. I help her look around her cabin, a cozy repository for her collection of sentimental keepsakes and comfortable old furniture, and, perhaps with the rosary her crown jewels, a beloved guitar. The place has a residue of good smells from recent home-cooked meals. We never find the rosary. She'll phone me hours later to say it was in the bottom of a basket in her van, not to worry.

Her house stands on raised pillars across the road from Butte La Rose Canal, a brown and meandering body of water that eventually oozes into Henderson Lake in Louisiana's magnificent Atchafalaya Swamp. It's a road lined mostly with weekend campsites for Cajun sportsmen and their families, camp houses with names like "Dad's Pad When Mom's Mad." I once kept my own houseboat, the *Green Queen*, on the canal and was privy to the road's seasonal changes. I marveled how it came alive with the first signs of spring. When temperatures rose above sixty, Cajuns sought the sun like so many lizards. The large Catholic families gathered at each of the small campsites to cook a little something and to drink a lot. Good times rolled.

Helen's raised red house also has a name, Camp Catahoula, for her birth town of Catahoula a few miles down the road. It is not really a camp in the vernacular sense, however, but her permanent home. The nicest one she's ever had. And she's proud of it. With good reason.

Camp Catahoula has one of the best screened porches I've ever been privileged to visit. On it are half a dozen cages that hold Helen's many mourning doves, white birds that remind you of the illustrations on old-fashioned valentines, coo-cooing in time to the music. There's a chifferobe, assorted potted plants that thrive under Helen's tutelage, baskets that others didn't want painstakingly painted by Helen and hanging from the ceiling. And there's an old radio that nine times out of ten is tuned to KBON, a Eunice, Louisiana, station that plays country and Cajun hits all day, every day. Including Helen's songs. The station plays Helen Boudreaux a lot, and no matter how many times I hear it, it startles me to recognize a friend on the radio.

When the Mississippi River began its historic rise in 2011, threatening the heavily populated Baton Rouge and New Orleans areas, the decision was made to open the Morganza Spillway. The Morganza was designed to divert flood water into the Atchafalaya River Basin, a good idea except for the poor souls who call it home. Helen and her neighbors were ordered to evacuate, and most did. Helen cheerfully hoisted her furniture and worldly goods to the ceiling, moved in with a daughter and went about her business. I never once heard her complain. She waited. And waited. And the worst did not happen. If it had, I feel certain Helene would have coped. She always has.

Helen's life has been hard, and she's the first to admit it. A lovely, Rubenesque redhead, she looks much younger than her seventy-two years, but has the sad and penetrating eyes of a woman who has seen too much too often for too long.

She had asthma as a child and that made her stand out, not in a good way, from among her mother's fourteen children. "I had asthma so severe I'd lose my breath walking across the street; no wonder my mother didn't like me," Helen concludes matter-of-factly.

Childhood wasn't all bad. There was that *place* of her childhood, for one thing, a paradise of live oaks strung with Spanish moss, the watery pathways called bayous that network like spider veins through the flat countryside. Helen has written rhapsodic songs about her peaceful hometown—"Ma Belle Catahoula" is the best paean. And she speaks glowingly of her father: "Papa worked hard in the fields; he provided for his children. If any of us learned common sense, it was from him . . ."

Somewhere along the way she developed a practical and fierce resilience that kept her red head above swamp water for, lo, these seventy years. And the mere act of survival has kept the Cajun chanteuse proud.

"I have fished crawfish, run trout lines and crab traps, shrimped in the Gulf. It took me two weeks to tear down an abandoned cypress frame house I bought for $350, and that included the fireplace. With the materials, I added three rooms to a mobile home in Butte LaRose and rebuilt the fireplace. I dug dirt and installed my own sewer system. I bought a five hundred-gallon septic tank, fifty feet of sewer pipes and a black tarp." With her then fifteen-year-old son as assistant, a shovel for digging and a hatchet to cut roots, Helen dug a fifty-three-foot field line, fifteen inches deep.

"In years past I bought a cow and milked it myself for my eight kids. I grew my own garden . . ."

She's raised those eight children, mostly alone, the best she could. Among her litany of regrets is the fact she stayed with an abusive husband, her second of four, a subject she wrote about exhaustively in her sad little book called, of course, *Cajun Survivor*.

Through it all, she sang. She sang when she worked in her sharecropper father's fields cutting cane, picking peppers and cotton. She sang when she and her first husband, a soldier, were stationed in faraway Hawaii and he spent far too much time at the NCO club, drinking. He would pretend not to know her when, to the delight of everyone else, the gorgeous young redhead took the stage. She sang through the bruises and aches when her second husband, a respected school teacher with a Jekyll and Hyde personality, made life miserable with what Helen says were constant harsh beatings and threats that were anything but idle. She sang when she finally mustered the courage to leave with the kids and try to make it on her own. She sang during her ten-year career as a truck driver, maneuvering the blue Peterbilt with its pink appointments across the country countless times. And, after she hurt her back and had to stop driving, she sang to make a living.

When she sings, it is sometimes in English, sometimes in French. And often, whether in English or French, it is one of Hank's songs she is singing. Hank's songs have been a mainstay in her repertoire, the eggs in her pound cake. And to hear Helen Boudreaux sing a Hank Williams song in French is as near to a heaven as there is, I'm convinced.

She first heard Hank when she was about nine, in her Catahoula childhood home, or perhaps beneath it, where she often played while listening to the radio. One day Hank's voice, that startlingly unique voice, came down through the heavens, through the wire antenna attached to the roof, winding through the window to the old chest-of-drawers that held a big battery and a little radio. Helen was smitten. And that memorable day began the only one of her romances that would last a lifetime, never turn sour and sustain her in tough times. Hank, unlike every other man she ever loved besides her beloved Papa, never let her down.

"We had that battery-operated radio, and after it would be on a while, it would fade in and out. We kids had to be very quiet lying on the floor so we would not miss the music. I remember my parents would say, 'Sa voix est beau!' [His voice is handsome!]

"At the time I discovered Hank's voice, we were so French I could not connect with his words, but I did with his voice. I'd listen for his singing on the radio. It did not matter what he sang, just so I could hear his singing . . .

"I could not sing along or follow his voice. I either had to sing too high, which would make me hoarse, or sing too low. So I'd compromise by singing to 'fit in' with his voice, like zigzagging with him through his songs. I learned a trick with my vocals. I did not know at the time what harmonizing meant, but that's what it was."

By the time she was ten, Helen's older siblings were in school and speaking some English at home. Parish teachers insisted that only English be spoken in school. Slowly she understood more of Hank's heartfelt lyrics, words which gave her a second jolt—with that beautiful music and voice came poetic words. "So many of his songs were down-to-earth experiences. I connected his lyrics with my own kinfolks."

When young Helen awoke each morning, she'd pull an old rocker missing an arm to the east window of the family's house that overlooked Catahoula Lake. "When the sun began to show above our Cousin Mae's oak trees, I knew then it was time for the music to start on the radio . . . Because my legs were too short to reach the floor, I would pull the rocker close to the window. I sat on the edge of the rocker and that way I could push against the window with my feet while holding onto the one good arm . . . Finally a faint sound would begin coming from the radio . . . Then, slowly the music got louder and louder. The music came up, and a man would talk . . . I thought all these people were inside the radio and were each taking their turns to talk and sing. I was so happy there in my own little world that sometimes it felt as though my heart would burst. But then, after eight or nine songs, sounds from the radio would begin to fade away, and after a while it would fall silent. The battery had faded out . . ."

But Hank was in her heart and hasn't ever faded away. His presence only grew stronger, with more wattage than the most powerful station.

"Eventually when we did get electricity and Mama bought a radio, and with good airwaves, we'd hear Hank on the late-night radio shows in New Mexico, Texas, Cincinnati, and New Orleans."

Nobody seemed to love a living Hank more than the Cajuns. It might have had something to do with his appearances on the *Louisiana Hayride*. You might say the start of his great fame began in Shreveport, where the show took place. First rattle out of the box, at his *Hayride* debut in 1948, Hank sang "Move It On Over" and everyone went wild. "Hank Williams's fame via the *Louisiana Hayride* sealed the radio show's status as a forum from which hopeful country musicians of the post-war era could gain exposure and success . . .," writes music historian Tracey E. W. Laird in the definitive history of the show, *Louisiana Hayride: Radio and Roots Music Along the Red River*. To get on the show, Hank had to convince KWKH management he could remain sober for six months, an odd enough arrangement anywhere but downright bizarre considering the broadcast was in Louisiana. Later, after the *Opry* let Hank go for the unreliability that rode tandem with his drinking, he came back to the *Hayride* to perform, a moment of irony if ever there was one.

You might say Hank's career began and ended with a pepper-hot Cajun embrace.

Or, it could be the Cajuns loved him so much because he went to the trouble to write in their patois in the great song "Jambalaya." Almost immediately it became a Cajun national anthem, second only to "Jolie Blonde" as a Louisiana crowd-pleaser. One of the first songs he ever recorded was "On the Banks of the Old Ponchartrain," not Hank's finest musical moment, but his first public connection to Louisiana.

And later Hank married a Louisiana woman, chose her from the multitudes, you might say. When Hank could have had anybody, he went to the well at Bossier City, wedding Billy Jean Jones, the comely daughter of a police officer who had lived down the street from Hank and Audrey during his first *Hayride* run.

More important to the Cajun love connection, I believe, was Hank's guileless nature. It takes one to know one, as they say. For my money the most pleasing of all Cajun characteristics is a total lack of pretense; some would substitute the word "honesty." Hank Williams told it like it was.

Hank's songs were about rudimentary things that poor but honest people understand best, be they Cajuns, crackers, hillbillies, or Knob Hill snobs. Love, loss, death, betrayal. He sang about the verities. Ol' Hank had been there, done that, bought the whole damn T-shirt factory. You could just tell by the timbre of his voice, the soulful register of his yodel, his simple words. His music resonated in a way that pop music and Big Band orchestras and even lots of other country songs did not.

Helen wasn't the only Cajun singer to find Hank. Vin Bruce, one of the first Cajuns to work the *Grand Ole Opry* and record with bigtime Nashville musicians like Chet Atkins and Owen Bradley, was born in 1932 in Cut Off, Louisiana, where he lives to this day, surrounded by his children and grandchildren. When Vin was a boy, his father played Cajun fiddle for local dances, and Vin taught himself to sing and play guitar so he could tag along. By age fourteen, Vin had joined Dudley Bernard and his Southern Serenaders band.

After he struck out on a solo career and began writing his own songs, Vin's work caught the attention of Columbia Records, with whom he signed in 1951. Vin met Hank by happy accident in Nashville in 1951. Vin Bruce was only nineteen years old, shopping for a belt in Hank & Audrey's Corral, one of many money-making ventures that Hank tried his hand at to pacify his ambitious first wife. Vin was walking around the big city, all eyes and excitement, when he saw the Corral. He tells the story, sixty years later, in a delightful Cajun accent.

"I had finished a recording session, and I told my manager I was going to take a walk. My first stop was the Corral. I walked in and saw some belts. I thought to myself, 'Let me ask if they could put my name on my belt.'"

They could put anything he wanted on the belt, the clerk bragged, so Vin waited. When the work was done, he walked to the cashier to pay for his purchase. Hank was coming from a small room in the back of the store. Vin was dumbstruck.

"'Oh, Lord,' I said. It's Hank Williams. Hank was the biggest. We almost bumped into each other. But it was Hank who talked to me, not the other way."

"What you got?" Hank asked the kid.

"I got a belt with my name on it," Vin stammered.

"Where are you from?" Hank asked.

"First I said 'New Orleans.'" He figured at least Hank had heard of that. "Then I said, 'Really, I'm from south of New Orleans. Cut Off.' And that's when he really warmed up. It was a real coincidence . . ."

Hank was supposed to perform in Cut Off soon, a place called Belleview Hall, near where Vin lived. The younger man told Hank he'd just finished a Columbia recording session, which impressed Hank and prolonged the conversation. The superstar invited the boy to stop by and see him when he made it to Louisiana. So, of course, Vin did.

It was after that Cut Off performance that Hank invited Vin and his band to open the two extravagant shows that would double as Hank's public wedding to Billie Jean Jones, then a voluptuous Louisiana teenager, long red hair and big breasts, who showed up with Faron Young at the *Opry* one night.

I asked Vin Bruce if Billie Jean was as stomp-down gorgeous as everyone says—and all the photographs indicate.

"Oh, I could have married her myself, and she was older than me," Vin recalls. "After Hank died, I was playing and traveling a lot and she joined me in performances a couple of times."

For a while after Hank's death, there were two Mrs. Hank Williams performing—Billie Jean and Audrey. Nobody seemed to notice. Audrey and Hank's mother soon coerced the young widow into accepting a $30,000 payoff to fade into the background, and that effectively eliminated one Mrs. Hank Williams. For a time.

A year after Hank's death, Vin Bruce would play for his hero again, this time in the Montgomery cemetery when they unveiled the monument that marks Hank's grave. The Montgomery radio station used the occasion for a big promotional to-do. "It was different this time from playing at his wedding," Vin says. "Chills went all over me, and the sweat was coming out all over."

Vin Bruce, now nearing eighty, is still marveling over the lasting influence of Hank Williams.

"It's hard to explain . . . If you listen to his songs, the words were very simple. It wasn't big words like some songs use. I just went to the seventh grade, and that means a lot when you can put a song out that everybody can understand.

"The good Lord gives you a gift, you take it or leave it. That man could take a pencil and write it all in no time at all. Simple words and melodies that could make you cry. Everyone was on his side, and he used it."

The late Drifting Cowboy fiddler Jerry Rivers, arguably Hank's best friend, had a more cynical explanation of Hank's "simple words." He said in a 1984 interview with Pat and Don Grierson that Hank used simple words because that's what he knew.

Here was this guy with about a fifth-grade education. Some of the DJ's, even back then, were trying to put him into some mysterious, holy setting that he didn't understand. This DJ out in California asked him, "Hank, tell me how do you write such deep, sad songs with such deep life, like 'Cold, Cold Heart' and 'I'm so Lonesome I Could Dry'?" Hank said, "Aw, Cottonseed, I guess I always have been a *sadist*." So there you are. He didn't know what that meant, either. That wasn't humor. That was ignorance. He had seen that word somewhere and thought it meant just sittin' around sad all the time . . .

Makes for a good story. But I keep thinking it's not so simple to use the *right* simple word. As Mark Twain famously said, it's the difference between "lightning" and a "lightning bug."

As a child, I remember looking up "shackled" one day after I heard "Cold, Cold Heart" on the radio or television. I had no idea what it meant. And Mother had told us to look up words we heard that we didn't know, and to read with a dictionary in our lap. That's the only way you'll improve your vocabulary, she said. That's one bit of maternal advice I've always followed.

I still marvel at Hank's imagery in that one line. His lover's heart was "shackled to a memory." That's about the best four-word description of living in the past I've ever heard.

Hank lived his songs, or at least that's the conventional wisdom. If lyrics about heartache came easy, it's because he had it hard, had experienced it firsthand.

One day I asked Helen if she, similarly, used for fodder the troubles in her own troubled past. God knows she has plenty to choose from. Many of her songs are in French, so as much as I appreciate the beauty of her voice and melody, I often don't know exactly what she's singing about. Some just *sound* like they might be about pain.

"The songs I write are little made-up songs, or just songs about other people," she answers. "I walked away from hardship and bad luck, and I surely don't want to include that in my songs. I do not want to relive that part of my life in my songwriting I guess . . ."

And then she makes an amazing declaration, especially for a prideful woman who is as capable of professional vanity as the next artist. She has, in fact, waged a one-woman war for decades against discrimination that women in the music business find in the chauvinistic, anachronistic world that's called South Louisiana.

"Only Hank is a *real* songwriter. He has touched everyone, young and old alike, every walk of life. Hank makes me look into my own soul to try to imagine myself following his steps . . ."

Helen has won female vocalist and songwriting honors several times in the prestigious Cajun French Music Association contests, and has been, at the invitation of the French government, to the islands of St. Pierre and Miquelon to sing at an international women's conference. She's racked up dozens of other honors and awards, many attesting to her tireless efforts to keep her Cajun culture vibrant and intact.

Yet it's not usually her own songs that she sings when she records videos for YouTube. She sits on that lonely but lovely Louisiana porch she calls home and sings Hank Williams songs to the woods and the porch doves and the alligators and to the camera because, as she so honestly puts it: "Hank. That's what people really want to hear."

Only Hank.

CHAPTER SIX

"Back then people closed their eyes and listened to music."

— Neil Young

Falling for Flint McCullough, fearless scout on television's *Wagon Train*, might have been the first time my heart beat to music. I was four.

Music has always figured heavily into the great, and not-so-great, romances of my life, providing the score behind my inevitable lovelorn theatrics. I guess that makes me about as unique as gravel. As Mrs. Slocombe used to say on the British comedy series *Are You Being Served*, "I am unanimous in that."

It's interesting how each of my love affairs has had its own soundtrack—sometimes using an entire genre, sometimes an individual artist who dominated my mental airwaves. And when they were done, when the man was gone, well, then Hank sang the eulogy.

My family hadn't had its black and white television set long before I discovered those coffee eyes of Flint's and fell hard. I got an actual spanking for throwing my crayon box at the television set one night when Flint kissed a starlet. I knew the kiss was make-believe, if convincing, but I thought it would be cute to pretend otherwise, to pretend I was jealous. Cute, unfortunately, didn't extend to endangering appliances. Nothing broke, thank god. Mother had positioned her red and reclining oriental children television lamp on top of our set, and it's a small wonder I didn't miss the screen and break bric-a-brac; that would have been the end of me. Those Green Stamps didn't grow on trees.

Actor Robert Horton played Flint, with great verve and romance. The man knew how to wear fringe. I pretended that Flint and I were on the same wagon train that embarked each morning from the pink Pensacola patio that Daddy built. We weren't traveling from Missouri to California like the television's pilgrims. My wagon train hoped to get from Florida to Montana, a state I'd heard of for some reason, by Sunday.

Each morning after Captain Kangaroo locked up the Treasure House for the day, stuffing that enormous set of keys into the deep pockets of the world's first leisure suit, the wagon train broke camp. Wagons-ho! I'd settle myself atop a redwood picnic table and begin the day's long, arduous ride across the Great Plains. Flint would be about his scouting duties, always just out of sight as a good scout should be. I knew he was thinking about me, however, no matter what Indians or highway robbers or mountain lions he might encounter. If four-year-olds can have fantasies, albeit chaste ones, I did.

You cannot begin such a journey without music. I had many tunes to choose from to keep the Flint flame aglow. But my favorite then was "Love Letters (Straight from My Heart)" as sung by Nat King Cole: *"Keep us so near, while apart."* I sang the few words that I knew again and again while coaxing my team of horses across the prairies and through mountain passes that would have unnerved a lesser heroine. "Home on the Range" also seemed appropriate. And I wasn't above mixing musical metaphors with "The Ballad of Davy Crockett," celebrating another fringed hero.

Flint had staying power. Five seasons.

In third grade I dumped him for someone closer to my own age, a classmate named Dan Jones. He had the whitest blond hair I've ever seen, buzzed into the prettiest velvet crew cut imaginable. Dan Jones was one of the popular boys, along with Steve Murphy and a few others anointed at birth, I guess, to be grammar school royalty. "I Want to Hold Your Hand!"

didn't cover it. If only the Beatles had added: "And touch your hair!"

Dan and Steve were popular, in part, because they were stars of the Peewee football team, an off-campus, YMCA-sponsored initiation to the tough-guy sport. Girls who wanted to—most of us did—could become cheerleaders for the Y's Peewee teams; all you had to do was *show up* and *ante up* for a uniform. I went to a few practices, but Mother didn't sew and couldn't justify paying for a cheerleader outfit on our family's limited budget. Everything the cheerleading squad wore had to match—down to the tennis shoes. No variations on theme or color. God forbid you wear white Keds when navy blue ones were required. Mother didn't see the necessity of color-coding Peewee pep.

It begins early, the advantages of having lots of discretionary income. Peewee cheerleaders often went on to become junior high cheerleaders, who became high school cheerleaders, who either got pregnant or were part of the homecoming court, or both. Oh, what I missed. From the high hill of my old age, as some wise Indian said, I can see now that it's character-building to be deprived of some experiences. At the time, I thought Mother cruel. Now I think she was mostly right to protest the prissy concept of color-conforming outfits to be worn for an hour on about ten Saturday mornings in the fall. There had to be better uses for money.

But I do have to note, those grammar school rituals set the scene for life through high school. The bad boy in first grade never was allowed to reform. He became the high school hood. The Blue Bird reader became the Beta Club president. The cheerleaders became, well, the cheerleaders, ipso facto official campus beauties. I guess some of us had to fall between the cracks to fill out the Greek chorus. I was a Greek chorus kind of gal.

I must admit, even if I'd had the kind of mother who saw the necessity of mastering the cartwheel and the split, I didn't have the moves necessary to make a good cheerleader. I'd practice in the yard at home and think I was getting it: *VI. VI. VICT. TO. TO. TORY. V-I-C-T-O-R-Y. Victory!*

Victory! Victory! Yeah! It looked good when I performed by myself, but as soon as I stood in line with the other girls I grew nervous and fell out of sync. I was Lucy with bananas on my head, trying to fool Ricky while disguised as part of the Copacabana dance troupe. I basically was miserable standing front and center, exhorting a crowd to yell themselves silly for a game I did not understand.

Not that I wasn't somewhat athletic. I could ride a horse and hit a baseball and otherwise make grade as a tomboy, which I proudly claimed to be. It was the dance-style coordination I lacked, doing things in time to some invisible metronome. Having never taken the baby-step tap and ballet that other girls did, I was lost. I still blame that omission for not knowing what to do with my hands at cocktail parties and funerals.

By the sixth grade, my unrequited love for Dan Jones had exhausted every Beatles hit and a few of Herman's Hermits ditties. Some snitch told Dan I liked him, and to my everlasting surprise, smooth man Dan phoned the house one weekend evening, waking my entire family—which meant it had to be after 8 o'clock in the evening. I listened nervously as Daddy answered the phone in his grouchy telephone voice. He always insisted on answering at night lest some bogeyman jump through the phone line and bludgeon to death the entire family.

Dan brazenly asked my father if I could accompany him, Dan, to the movies, or perhaps it was the other way around. My parents were about as open to dating in the sixth grade as they would have been to coed martini overnights. My father said, flatly, "No. And don't you ever call here again."

Dan never did.

IN JUNIOR HIGH SCHOOL I fell madly in love with a goofy jock named Lee Gross, real name, who wasn't handsome like Flint or Dan, but who had self-assurance and personality in spades. By junior high standards, that meant telling scatological jokes with flair and charming teachers into passing grades. Lee's course as a super football jock already had been set, and it never once varied through high school or Auburn University, where he became an All-American center. He would go on to rear a son who was, briefly, Auburn's quarterback and later a professional baseball player.

Lee already had a girlfriend, of course, the popular and pretty Karen. Karen's skirts were shorter, her ponytail longer, her giggle more spontaneous, and her parents less strict. I didn't stand a chance.

Lee keeps me stringing—a rat in his pocket—by winking at me when we chanced to meet in the hallway and by sitting beside me at lunch period, whenever his lunch period wasn't the same as Karen's. One Valentine's Day he bought and brought me a small box of chocolates in the regulation cellophane-wrapped heart. He stood beneath the vapor light outside my house and said something romantic like, "Here. Got you one, too, kid. Gotta go."

I was on Cloud Nine until Karen made a point of telling me, and many others, she thought he'd been "sweet" to remember me. Her box was undoubtedly bigger with more soft centers.

My infatuation for Lee lasted, and lasted, through three years of junior high and off and on in high school. My musical preferences by then ran to smooth, harmony-heavy, collegiate groups, like The Lettermen. They sang "If I Fall in Love; It Will Be Forever." I put *my* money where *their* mouths were. I would be a freshman at Auburn before finally I got Lee out of my system for good. Poor Karen hung with the program even longer than I did, eventually being dumped by Lee when he married his Auburn Reading Improvement professor.

I really, really got over it a mere ten years after Lee and I sat side-by-side at high school graduation. It was a forced issue, in case you're wondering; we were seated alphabetically. Grimsley. Gross. He let me wear his class ring until the ceremony was over, when he sprinted for the door and party plans with Karen. I've only been to one high school reunion ever, my tenth. I was twenty-eight and thought I looked pretty good, that is, for me. So, naturally, I went. I was humming "The Way You Look Tonight" as I not so subtly searched for he-man Lee. He was busy looking for Karen.

MY FIRST BOYFRIEND IN college, Michael, was as square as a laptop. He was, in fact, majoring in computer science, what was called at the time "data processing." He lived in Cherry Trailer Park on Auburn's main artery, and we mostly watched G-rated television sitcoms when we got together. Though we might have gone to a campus concert or two—I think Ike and Tina was one cultural leap we made—music was not the glue in our relationship. Turns out, there was no glue in our relationship.

I was beginning to experiment, not with drugs but with music. In the dormitory getting ready for dates, I'd have my long hair full of electric rollers and enough goop on my face to lube a small engine. Aretha's "Natural Woman" would be blaring on somebody's stereo, and without a trace of irony I'd sing along while painting and buffing and otherwise rearranging myself. By then I'd discovered Bob Dylan and Elton John and watched the Woodstock movie twice. I wasn't a heavy metal type of girl, but I had left the Lettermen, never to return.

I remember parties after football games with Three Dog Night rocking the trailer. Jeremiah was a bullfrog, but Michael was no prince. The weekend it snowed, a la *Doctor Zhivago*, I met him on the sidewalk holding hands with his hometown honey, a ravishing blond. That was the beginning of the inevitable end. It was for the best. Michael's idea of a romantic date was going to Shoney's for strawberry pie after Sunday night service at the Baptist church. That kind of future-Jaycee behavior was hard to match with a love theme. And his politics were to the right of Ronald Reagan's, that Neanderthal governor of California who recently had been quoted as saying if you'd seen one redwood you'd seen them all.

Michael's father owned a furniture store, however, and for Christmas my sophomore year Michael gave me my first nice stereo. That was his major contribution to my music education, nothing at which to sneeze. I hauled that prize around long after I married, only to have its plastic dust cover melt all over my Leon Russell album when I set up the appliance too close to a wood heater in Counce, Tennessee.

Michael and I made attempts at being serious, but I don't think either of us could see it happening. Opposites may attract, but then kill each other over the television remote or the radio dial. I moved on.

Jimmy Johnson could dance. When Jimmy and I first got together, Jim Croce was singing my life. "Time in a Bottle" seemed to say it best.

When we married the next year the paid organist played my favorites: "Morning Has Broken," an old Methodist hymn Cat Stevens had made cool and popular; "Oh, What a Beautiful Morning," a Broadway favorite from my piano lesson days; and John Denver's "Sunshine on My Shoulders."

It was December, early morning. The music floated through the manicured woods of Georgia's Callaway Gardens, providing the perfect backdrop for a couple of poor lovebirds who still believed in newspapers comforting the afflicted and afflicting the comfortable, and in music soothing the soul.

And no matter our differences or problems, journalistic poverty being at the top of the list, music helped. It always helped. In our salad days we grazed a variety of genres—folk, rock and roll, progressive country, Motown, Frank Sinatra. By our thirties we'd found sailboats and Jimmy Buffett, another Alabama boy who filled a musical niche and lived a life we could only dream about. For a while, that's all we listened to. Buffett, expert lyricist, eventually would ask the great musical question: "What if the hokey-pokey was really what it's all about?"

But an evergreen on our playlist, atop the impressive stack of vinyl that made some seventeen moves in eighteen years, there was always Hank Williams, with that voice that sounded like our childhoods in working-class Alabama. Harold Johnson, Jimmy's father, had worked seven days a week in a textile mill so his boys wouldn't have to. Lera Johnson, Jimmy's mother, had worked at a beauty shop six days a week, and on the seventh day hadn't rested, but fixed hair for free at the local nursing home. When they talked about degrees, they meant the temperature outside, not the academic kind. They were democratic in every sense of the word. When Harold brought friends home from the mill to sit around the dinette and eat a good meal, the group included black and white men. He'd sit for hours with a cousin who ran the scales at the landfill, drinking and chewing the fat.

We were both from the same working stock as ol' Hank, only Hank lost his footing too soon, too young. And I think that without Hank, we might have lost ours, too. He lost his life that we might be saved, or something like that.

Hank himself didn't have much luck in the romance department. He famously and first married a woman with a cheating heart and a spending fist. In fairness to Audrey, Hank subscribed to the double standard in place for traveling men at the time, shacking up with groupies when the opportunity twisted his arm. But he seemed genuinely to long for a monogamous home front; you could hear that longing in his songs. His second marriage might have been different—Billie Jean, despite her come-hither looks, seemed devoted and mercifully, at the time, exhibited no singing aspirations. But the couple would only have two and a half months to love, honor, and cherish. The jury was still out on that love affair when Hank died.

A happy Hank would have been his gain and our loss. A happy man could not have written "I'm So Lonesome I Could Cry." The images would not have even occurred to a happy man with a healthy relationship. A happy man might have known how to set the woods on fire, but he wouldn't have been walking the floor or staring up at a purple sky. He wouldn't have been singing the blues.

I remember one late night when my divorce was imminent, headed toward home from some distant assignment, riding alone in a Mustang meant for two. I was in Tennessee, where AM radio at night usually aired one of two things: basketball or preaching. But this night I could hear a country station through the static. I could hear Hank. Must have been WSM, I'm not certain.

What I do remember for certain is that for the first time, I fully appreciated how ol' Hank articulated loss, better than anyone perhaps save Shakespeare, and in far fewer words. Hank had walked in my shoes.

Misery not only loves company, she needs for the company to sit up late drinking with her, commiserating, and reciting poetry. She needs for the company to sing her back home.

And Hank did.

CHAPTER SEVEN

"The problem that I've seen, especially when you start to get down around Montgomery, people are starting to create their own Hank Williams. 'Oh, yeah, he and I got drunk every night.' Everybody down there is his cousin, and every musician played in his band . . ."

— JERRY RIVERS, OF THE DRIFTING COWBOYS

The great football coach Vince Dooley was a young man, just a kid, really, playing football for Auburn, his alma mater, when he tore a cartilage during the 1952 Auburn-Ole Miss game. His knee would get better, then he'd hurt it all over again in the next game. Dooley endured a vicious cycle of injury and repair, injury and repair, which ultimately resulted in knee surgery after his senior football season.

He was stuck in a Montgomery hospital, recuperating from that surgery, spending three or four cold January days flat on his back, blue about the fact he was missing, of all things, *basketball* season. "I loved basketball, too," he says, "and that year when I went out for the basketball team I was encouraged, feeling about the fifth day like I was getting into the groove . . . I went stepping, the knee went out for the third time, so off I went. This day and time it could have been scoped, but the only way to solve it back then was to take the cartilage out."

His recuperation was made bearable by Hank's death.

"While I was in the hospital, they held Hank's funeral in Montgomery. I listened to it on the radio, and then for days afterward all they played was Hank, all day long . . ."

And that was fine by Dooley. So devout a Hank fan is he—now retired and cloaked in the usual armor of honors like any respected Southeastern Conference coach—that one of his proudest moments was being named an honorary Drifting Cowboy by the folks at Montgomery's Hank Williams Museum. Dooley had grown up in Mobile, listening to Hank and the *Opry*, loving all the hits, but especially "I Saw the Light." And they sang that one, of course, at Hank's funeral, as the injured young football star lay desolately listening.

Roy Acuff and Ernest Tubb and Red Foley and other *Opry* stars said goodbye to Hank in song, and a crowd overflowed Montgomery's city auditorium, milling about the cold street in silence and despair.

Nobody really saw it coming, the outpouring. Biographer Paul Hemphill noted that by the time of Hank's death there had been only four mentions of him in the Nashville newspapers. Yet Hank drew a crowd in death, same as life. I have seen half a dozen estimates of the number of mourners, anywhere from three thousand to one hundred thousand. The most authoritative put the figure at about twenty thousand, gathered there in and around city hall; a statue of Hank now stands in a park-like space across the street.

More important than the number was the *mood* of those who gathered. I envision it as being like that scene in *Close Encounters of the Third Kind*, when disparate strangers from all over show up independently because they've been spoken to at different times by the same alien force. They are all amazed that others felt compelled to come, to gather as a whiz-bang spaceship makes its landing. Hank's songs were so personal that each and every fan thought he might be the only one there, a Jay Gatsby funeral.

Even the family was shocked. "I was at the funeral with Aunt Lilly," Hank's cousin Taft Skipper told journalist Larry Powell. "That was the first time we realized he was as famous as he was. We had to have an escort away from the city auditorium."

That Sunday funeral that Vince Dooley heard from his hospital bed was just one last public event for an essentially private man. It followed his wedding to Billie Jean Jones seventy-four days earlier. There's big time irony there in Hank's public airing of things most stars strain to keep private: marriage and memorial. And basically it went against Hank's nature, too.

"He kept a lot of things to himself, and was a very private person," musician Boots Harris told Pat Grierson. Harris was an *Opry* member and the first steel guitarist to perform on the Ryman stage. He died in 2003. As a young man, age seventeen, Boots Harris played steel guitar with an early incarnation of the Drifting Cowboys. He knew Hank at eighteen, long before Hank was a star, before Audrey and the *Opry* and Billie Jean. But, Harris admitted, nobody knew Hank all that well.

> I doubt if anyone ever really knew all of him. I had only known him for an hour, and he conned me into buying him a half pint. He loved the effect it had on him. He wasn't too temperamental. Later on, he might have been . . . He had a tremendous drive. It consumed him. In Montgomery we would go to juke joints, and he'd say, "Someday my music will be on there." He was just a teenager then, but he had a real sense of destiny . . . He was convinced he wanted to make records, to hear them on the jukebox, and to get up on stage. That was about all he ever wanted—besides Audrey and the money . . .

PRIVATE PERSON THAT HE was, Hank had to eat. And after the divorce from Audrey and being fired from the *Opry*, it was a little like starting over. Public matrimony was a promoter's idea.

There had been three Louisiana "weddings" in all: one that counted and two ostentatious public ceremonies at the New Orleans Municipal Auditorium, a matinee at 3 o'clock and another at 7. The public events were purely for show and the money. It is said Hank took home about

$15,000 for his trouble. Hank, some swear, was worried that Audrey might try to disrupt the highly advertised public weddings. So the night before the scheduled Sunday, October 19 shows, Hank and Billie Jean borrowed a car from her brother and headed to nearby Minden, Louisiana, where they were married by a justice of the peace. They gave out of gas on the way back to New Orleans.

Most of Hank's devoted fans clearly embraced the romantic notion of their Lovesick Boy finding love again, especially in the curvaceous form of the redheaded and ravishing Billie Jean. Both shows sold out. There were crates of champagne, a five-foot wedding cake, and Hank almost outshone the bride in his snow-white cowboy hat, black duds with bright green fringe and white trim. Souvenir wedding programs were sold. Posters advertised that every ticket holder would be a guest at the "beautiful, solemn ceremony joining in holy wedlock Miss Billie Jones and Hank Williams . . ."

But it was more three-ring circus than double-ring ceremony.

"The town of New Orleans gave me a trousseau—which I didn't even know what a trousseau was," Billie Jean told Hank enthusiast and author Brian Turpen. By day an Indiana police major, Turpen has made it his hobby to unearth little-known Hank tidbits and bills himself a "Hank researcher." In 2010 he compiled a photo book with essays called *Hank Williams & Billie Jean Jones: A Country Music Wedding Extravaganza*. And if ever a wedding deserved more attention, it's probably this double-decker.

"Some have claimed that Hank hoped Audrey would show up to stop the wedding, but the day's photos tell a different story," Turpen writes. "Hank and Billie appeared to be very happy. Billie Jean was radiant in her ankle-length white wedding gown, and Hank looked younger than he had in years, despite his thinning hair. Accounts note his weight at twenty-five to thirty pounds more than he weighed just a few months prior to the wedding. Billie claimed it was because Hank was eating decently for the first time in years, especially enjoying her mother's cooking . . ."

The author prides himself on using police skills honed at the Bedford Police Department to undercover rare Hank stories, shoe-leather techniques "to beat the bushes, look under the rocks," as he says. "I think more importantly I'm interested in the topic and want to know everything I can . . ."

Turpen has written, sometimes in exhaustive detail, about everything from Hank's older brother, born prematurely and dead in two days, to the *Opry* troupe's tour of Germany and Hank's use of catsup on foreign food.

People have been writing Hank books since the star died. Lillian Stone, for one, quickly penned her version of Hank's life and cast herself in a heroine's role. The late Jerry Rivers, Hank's fiddler player and friend, wrote his book in 1967, which, he said, sold "like wildfire," tens of thousands of copies. *From Life to Legend* was revised in 1980.

Rivers, who talked with Pat and Don Grierson, obviously already had grown weary of being interviewed about Hank. "For the last two or three [Hank] books I've wondered, you know, what else there might be to say about Hank," he complained. "I've done so many [interviews], I'm saying the same thing over and over."

He wrote his book, he said, for the same reason Hank wrote songs:

> To make some money. Even more so, [Hank wrote] to have a song that was bigger than somebody else's. He was very competitive. He was in this business, he wrote those songs for the same reason Tom T. Hall writes them. The same reason that Harlan Howard writes them. I've been here all my life. I've watched this business grow . . . from when the *Opry* paid seven dollars and now they pay 250 for a song . . . They can't kid me, they sit out there and write these songs to make money. They can tell me about they sat up one night and

had a vision, the Lord came down and gave 'em a song. But they did it to make money . . .

AN ENDLESS SERIES OF yard sales defined my forties. I'm not particularly proud of that, but somehow buying the discards of others became my poison of choice, and I couldn't get enough of other folks' rejects. I don't know about "chic," but my household certainly was shabby. At some point, even yard sales became too elegant for my contrarian taste, and I started braking for curbside plunder, most usually furniture.

My rural Georgia home had nearby a big green dumpster where each household hauled their trash, and spray-painted on the side of the big bin were the words, "Don't dive, Cracker." Whenever Don and I would be riding along and I'd sing out, "Stop, there's a perfectly good utility table," or some such, Don would oblige but always add with a smirk: "Don't dive, Cracker."

One day at a yard sale I purchased a big box of family photographs, not my family's pictures, you understand, but some unknown family's collection of sepia memories. It was a real find. There were babies in elaborate christening gowns held by old women in lace collars. There were two nuns in habits looking stern and devoted, plus dozens of pictures of children with their cowlicks slicked, their skirts and shirts starched, all posing for the sake of posterity.

I asked the woman running the yard sale how she could bear to part with such personal treasures, and I'll never forget her answer. "I have no idea who those people are, honey," she said, "Take them and enjoy."

And so I did. I stuck those old anonymous photos on my homemade valentines, and used them as Christmas card tags on packages. Somebody else's darlings flew here and yon, nameless faces recycled for my convenience.

That box of photos reinforced my belief that the dead do not linger forever, or even for very long. Few of us mortals ever manage to scratch our names onto that blackboard of life, the one that gets erased every Friday. We come, we see, we fail to conquer. We never get out of this world alive.

Hank is one of those rare exceptions. His name has grown bigger each and every year with song royalties to prove it, and there have been almost sixty of those years since his death.

I used Google to find a chronological list of "celebrity" deaths in 1953. It was long. Hank was at the top, of course, dying as he did on January 1. Most of the other hundred or so "celebrities," I'd never heard of. There were a few exceptions.

I'd heard of Jim Thorpe, of course, the Olympic gold medalist who died a month after Hank. And in March of that same year Josef Stalin went away—"Responsible for eleven million murders" is a credential with staying power. I also had heard of Dooley Wilson, who played it again while playing Sam in "Casa Blanca." The Rosenbergs, Ethel and Julius, were executed in '53. And I recognized the name Dylan Thomas, of course.

Most of the "celebrities" who died the same year as Hank were as anonymous now as the photographs in my yard sale box. They once were *somebodies*, too, and not so long ago. On the list were composers and authors and actresses—even a president and premier or two. Unrecognized, at least by me, were politicians and cinematographers and one Man Mountain Dean, a professional wrestler. Charles Gordon Curtis, inventor of the Curtis steam turbine, something useful it would seem, was there. As was Algy Gehrs, Australian cricketer. Larry Shields, American jazz clarinetist. Margaret Bondfield, feminist.

Despite what I'm sure were extraordinary contributions to the world of art, government, music, and theater by these men and women of note, death meant death for most. There would be no evergreen royalties for songs, no movies made about them, no biographies penned, no fan clubs established. They were gone. And forgotten.

HANK, ON THE OTHER hand, has survived. It might have been an uphill battle. There was Audrey's tawdry widow act right after his death, not to mention her maudlin attempts to market Bocephus as Hank incarnate. There were persistent and snide suggestions that Fred Rose wrote all of Hank's songs. And then there was that awful movie, *Your Cheatin' Heart*, starring the *other* Sun King, George Hamilton. You would have thought no mere mortal could have staged a resurrection from beneath the dirt they heaped onto Hank.

Then, of course, there was Elvis. He stampeded onto the cultural stage two years after Hank's death, changing the popular music scene forever with rock and roll. That entire genre became a catering service to youth. Suddenly traditional country music was about as hip as your father's galoshes. But somehow, despite all the above, Hank has weathered the toughest test of all: the test of time.

It's true. A lot of us put Hank beneath the bed for a while, or in a cedar chest where the moths wouldn't get to him, pulling him out when we needed a certain kind of solace, familiar warmth. I reached for him in south Alabama, remembering how I'd like his sour mash voice and the ache in his words. I wrote a newspaper feature story about an old fiddler, George Frye, who invited me to play my accordion at nursing homes where he entertained the prisoners every weekend. I figured nobody on the scene would report this decidedly uncool act to my friends. Living in Monroeville was like living on another planet, one with barely enough music to sustain life.

Mister Frye and I would set up in the dining hall of the nursing home, unfolding our chairs and opening our instrument cases. I'd strap on the showy blue accordion, and George would rosin his bow. And then, being the leader, he'd tap his toe three times and we'd launch into a tortured version of "Black Mountain Rag" or "Orange Blossom Special." I faked it, of course, with a few chords and a slapdash melody, until Mister Frye would tap us into a Hank song. I could keep up then, and I played louder and with more assurance. I couldn't help but notice that's when our audience would respond as well, adjusting their hearing aids and rolling their wheelchairs in a little closer.

None of the old folks there—and it was a religious place, Monroeville—seemed to mind the conventional wisdom that Hank had died in his cups with drugs in his system and a Dr. Feelgood at his beck and call. And they sure didn't seem to worry about where he got his tunes, or how it was that an unschooled boy wrote such pure poetry.

In his interview with Pat Grierson, the great Nashville songwriter Tom T. Hall made a good point about those pernicious questions that periodically swirl around the authorship of Hank's songs, usually in academic circles, or among jealous and inferior musicians. Same as the debates about Shakespeare and his writing. How could one man have done all that, and so quickly?

> If we believed all the Hank Williams street stories we have heard, it would lead us to the conclusion that he did not write the songs. We would understand that he bought them, accepted them as gifts and lifted the rest from books of poems. We would then have to wonder what wonderful magnetism drew these good and great pieces of work to the feet of this one man.
>
> I have sat over warm beer and faced bad company in ill-lighted places and listened to stories of how one writer or another managed his fame by purchase of great work from otherwise stupid people. It's frightening. If a song has Hank Williams's name on it, I render that song unto Mr. Williams. As I would turn loose a killer if the circumstantial evidence were overwhelming. No blood or wet ink on my hands . . .

That's absolutely right. How wonderful if you're in the business of stealing or buying songs that some Music Fairy delivers only the best stuff for you to regurgitate. How perfectly nifty.

No, most of us know instinctively that Hank wrote the songs with his name on it, a couple of exceptions duly noted by painstaking research and a discography of the Country Music Foundation Library and Media Center. Same way we know that cows give milk and clouds pour rain. Hank gave us good music, and nobody can take it away.

CHAPTER EIGHT

"You have brought music back into my life.
I had forgotten."

— CAPTAIN VON TRAPP IN *The Sound of Music*

During intermission at the movie *The Sound of Music*, I rushed
to the ladies' restroom of the Paramount Theater in downtown
Montgomery and tried to imagine my hair all cut off and styled
in a blond pixie like Julie Andrews's. It was a stretch, considering I had
long dark hair pulled tight from my forehead in a ponytail, the better to
look like Lori Martin in the television show *National Velvet* inspired by
the movie starring Elizabeth Taylor.

Not for long. I got it all cut off the next opportunity. And though I
looked nothing whatsoever like Julie Andrews, but more like Kim Darby as
Mattie in the original *True Grit*, I kept it short until I saw Vanessa Redgrave
as Queen Guinevere in *Camelot* two years later. Then I grew it out again.

Such was the influence of movies, especially musicals, during my
childhood in the 1950s and '60s. I didn't just watch the screen, lick the
butter from the buttered popcorn off my fingers, and enjoy the story and
characters for what they were—story and characters. I wanted to live the
story and *become* the characters. I was fickle, adopting the parts I had last
seen, forgetting all about last year's heroine, making it possible to morph
from a singing nun in the Austrian Alps to a disgraced, adulterous queen
tied to a stake in Camelot without passing Go.

I knew all the words to all the songs. I sang them at the top of my lungs
while swinging in the back yard, or riding my bicycle up and down, up

and down, neighborhood streets. Our suburban Montgomery hills came alive with the sound of music. Those songs from the musicals remain with me like piano recital pieces or scars from bike wrecks. To this day I cannot write the date on a check in the month of May without singing—usually not aloud—"It's May. It's May. The lusty month of May."

Judy Land was the only friend who could match me in the romantic soul department. She and I usually went together to musicals, reinforcing one another's fantasies about someday living in France or England, in some land where people ran through fields of wildflowers and burst into song at the least provocation. Judy was the most self-assured child I ever knew, and she didn't mind showing off her lovely soprano in public.

I know some otherwise reasonable folks who hate musicals. I find it hard to believe the ambivalent ever saw Franco Nero as Lancelot in *Camelot*, or Sam Woo winning his true love in *Flower Drum Song*. Or Richard Harris exhorting the young messenger boy to run "Behind the lines!" at the end of *Camelot, after* his paradise has gone to hell, his wife and best friend have made of him the most public of cuckolds, and the Round Table is kaput. From the lowest, darkest time of his life, Arthur/Richard Harris goes to the trouble to urge an idealistic boy to remain safe, and finds in the lad's determination to become a knight a glimmer of hope. If your heart doesn't break when Harris croakingly slides into the movie's last rendition of the title song, gradually gaining steam into a rousing refrain, I don't want to have a beer with you.

A movie didn't have to be a musical to have memorable music. I could whistle "Mammy's Theme" from *Gone With the Wind* if you asked me to. Not that you would, but I could. I didn't so much go to a movie as inhabit it. I've never bought curtains that I didn't imagine how they'd look made into a dress. I've never applied nail polish without humming "I Enjoy Being a Girl." Every fire escape in every alley makes me sing "Maria." Every time a wedding preacher asks if anyone has any objection to the vows being finalized, I half expect to look to the back of the church and see Dustin Hoffman banging on the stained glass screaming "Elainnnnnnnne!"; it's hard not to break into a stanza of "Mrs. Robinson."

Movies seen by today's kids cannot possibly have the same impact *our* movies had on my generation. We saw so relatively few. Fewer than today's youngsters certainly, and, surprisingly, fewer than our parents before us. We saw them once, forever and ever amen, not dozens of times, making them magical, not routine. Why is it that now I can see a movie three times on television reruns and not remember it as well as a movie I saw once fifty years ago? Movies then were more like solar eclipses, or the Northern Lights. In their rarity, they had major impact.

When my parents came of age, movies were cheap and there were no televisions. So they went to the movies a lot. It was an economical evening out. It might be the one luxury they had more of than we did. Even Hank Williams, from a family so poor he sold peanuts on the street, often talked about all the movies he saw in south Alabama.

We Boomers didn't see two or three films every week while growing up. And we certainly weren't privileged with movies from cable, satellite, Blockbuster, Netflix, Redbox, and dozens of other sources available today.

If you went to a movie, it was an occasion. A tremendously big deal. You sat in your Sunday clothes—I remember the blue velvet dress I wore to see *Camelot*, a hand-me-down from cousin Marilyn Jo—in comfortable upholstered seats and fidgeted until the lights dropped and the music reached a crescendo. You didn't utter a word once the previews began.

Choices were limited, and therefore important, because a movie might set your mood for the remainder of the year, or a lifetime. *Ole Yeller* broke my heart. Ditto *Spencer's Mountain. Camelot*—might for right—did a lot to set in stone, like the sword, my social conscience. *The Blob* made me afraid to open my closet. And, yes, though I'm almost ashamed to admit it, *Your Cheatin' Heart* broke my heart.

Jett Williams admitted the same in her book. When she saw that movie, she cried. Not because the movie was about her father; she had no idea at the time. But because the hero died in the end and you were supposed to cry. The dog *always* died in the end, and sometimes the human hero did, too. I've tried to rent the movie and watch it again, for research purposes, but it's one of the rare omissions on Netflix. (I think Billie Jean's lawsuit might keep it out of circulation. The movie made no mention of Hank's divorce and remarriage, which Billie Jean successfully claimed defamed her.)

THE REAL HANK, NOT smarmy George Hamilton, had a close brush with becoming a movie star. MGM Pictures offered, and he signed, a four-year contract to make horse operas in the universal style of singing cowboys Gene Autry and Tex Ritter. And, frankly, it's not so hard to imagine ol' Hank on horseback, yodeling the "Lovesick Blues." He was a great entertainer, after all, and at ease in front of a microphone or camera.

Hank's heart wasn't in Hollywood, however, and anyway at a major planning session with studio brass he got drunk and made such an ass of himself that MGM tore up the contract.

Hank presumably resented the personal changes Hollywood demanded—and some he feared coming. A toupee for his balding head. A tutor to clean up his grammar. A voice coach to make him sound less country. He knew instinctively he was better off on the juke box than the silver screen.

"Look what they thought they had to do when they made the movie *Your Cheatin' Heart*," poet Miller Williams once said. "They had to change the voice and the instrumentation even then because they were embarrassed by it."

Hank's way with an audience might or might not have translated to movies; we'll never know. But it's hard to imagine him memorizing someone else's lines. If nothing else, he was an original. And he knew it. Deep down, he knew it. What's more, he knew his audience: the working man, the heartsick woman, the farmer whose major weekly entertainment remained the *Opry* on the radio. He knew his audience, and they knew him.

Biographer Paul Hemphill wrote that in 1951, the week before Hank was scheduled to be a guest on *The Perry Como Show* in New York, he played the Wagon Wheel Club on the main road between Opelika and Auburn, a cinderblock dance hall with its signature wheel lit up with colored lights. High church and low church, but you can guess which was which in Hank's estimation.

It wasn't that Hank couldn't work a more sophisticated audience as well as Franco Nero or Richard Harris. He could. He had, after all, performed with other *Opry* stars in some of the great opera halls and theaters in post-war Germany and Austria, including the Titania Palast in Berlin. Brian Turpen, in his 2007 book *Ramblin' Man,* includes a wonderful remark Hank made when asked if the Germans liked his music: "Like it? Hell, they're more hillbilly than I am. We oughta move over there and open a damn record store."

It didn't matter if he sang in a palace or a dive where the band needed helmets. He wanted to see his audience, and feel their love, if you will.

Hugh Harris, who for a while now has made his living playing Hank, loves a story he heard from Drifting Cowboy Don Helms. "Hank was working a package show with Hank Snow and some others. I believe the venue was Houston [It was Dallas] . . . At show time, Hank was drunk and unable to perform. The other acts went on, stalled, killed time, apologized. But the audience wouldn't leave. About 2 a.m., Hank walked on stage, said, 'Good morning, folks,' and got a standing ovation . . . We'll never see the likes of him again."

The consensus from those who performed with Hank was that he had 'em by the heart. "He had a monstrous talent," Chet Atkins told the

Griersons. "He went out on the stage and would sway and sing. He could simply just charm the folks. He would sing one or two songs on the *Opry* stage. They just slayed the audience; they were gasping . . ."

Hank had that star quality that most of us don't, played that Pied Piper tune that could make a little girl want to cut off her ponytail in a theater restroom or become a nun. He knew it, he milked it, honed it. And sixty years later, the world is still feeling it.

CHAPTER NINE

"Only those with no memory insist on their originality."
— Coco Chanel

Hugh Harris is a short, wiry fellow, not someone you'd pick out of a lineup as a Hank Williams impersonator, or an Angola Prison guard. He's been both.

Hugh and his former wife had been married within a few months of the same length of time Hank and Audrey were married—seven years, give or take a wild-and-hairy separation or two. Then, as if following formula, the Hugh Harrises, too, divorced. Their only child, son Hardy, was about the same age as Hank Jr. was when his famous parents split. Let's hope the Harris marriage was a little more harmonious than Hank and Audrey's. But the details of its death were eerily similar.

"It was a very hard and negative time for me, and after doing those calculations, I remember telling my mother: 'I never wanted to be *this* much like Hank,'" Hugh says.

Maybe that's just a hazard of the Hank impersonating trade. Long hours. Road trips. Rowdy friends. Adoring fans. All can add up to marital friction. Now I know nothing of the details of Hugh's divorce, or, for that matter, Hank's. Most biographers paint Audrey the villain, but I'll play devil's advocate. It had to be hard living with the first country music superstar, especially when he was on the road and the bottle so much. It would make you, well, restless, and by all accounts Audrey was.

Even though he never planned on imitating Hank's marital discord, Hugh probably couldn't help but make note. It's one of those perverse ways of looking at your own fate and finding a degree of comfort in sharing it with someone you admire. You think to yourself: "Yep. That's it. My divorce shares statistics with ol' Hank's." Just one more dimension to the Hugh Harris Hank act.

For whenever he puts on his 1940s' suit and necktie and boots and a big cowboy hat that adds inches and helps the illusion, when he sings those familiar songs, Hugh becomes Hank. That has to be an on-the-edge kind of experience. Channeling troubled talent.

Hugh Harris has been feeling that weird rush for three decades. "The first time I knowingly heard Hank was as part of my kindergarten graduation program," the Louisiana native says. "We did 'Jambalaya' for one of our songs, and I went home singing it one afternoon. My mother heard me, and said, 'I have a record of that.'"

What she had was a copy of MGM's *Hank Williams' Greatest Hits*, which Hugh says he played "until the grooves were gone." Hooked on Hank, bolstered by family, he began playing the guitar about the same time as his kindergarten Hank epiphany. Dressing up and acting came naturally for the boy, and a neighbor once told Hugh's mother she could always tell what the child was pretending by what he was wearing. "I had to have my props, so I might go through four outfits in a day. The neighbor would see me in my football uniform; a little while later, a cowboy hat and holsters; still later, an Army helmet, and so on. Hats, Sunday suits, and a guitar constituted another set of props, and I needed it all if I were going to sing you a Hank Williams song."

At times playing Hank is a lot more lucrative than others, and he's had to keep the day job, but he's stuck with it, to great effect. I first saw Hugh play Hank at the old-timey Liberty Theater in Eunice, Louisiana, a restored, 1924 vaudeville playhouse where every Saturday night they do a kind-of Cajun French *Grand Ole Opry* called the *Rendez-Vous des Cajuns*. Imagine Ernest Tubb fed on gumbo, Roy Acuff without a tight ass. The show not only has hot Cajun bands, but often Cajun comedians and writers and the occasional cook. The live performance accommodates those in the audience who want to dance, and that's usually a whopping percentage of the crowd. Everybody not on walkers, anyhow. This is a free-spirited experience, Cajuns and tourists who often wear shirts or caps that say: *Laissez les bon temps rouler*. So the theater sprinkles a little sawdust on the wooden floor at the front of the auditorium, and, voila, a dance floor. I once saw a couple of seniors with his and her oxygen tanks waltzing across Texas at the Liberty.

Once a year, on the weekend nearest New Year's and thus Hank's death, the Liberty suspends the *Rendez-Vous* and regular programming to substitute a Hank Williams tribute. I've seen the Hank show at least seven times, wondering each time if they will have run out of good material and credible acts. So far, they have not. Before the show begins, the vintage auditorium is darkened and Hank Williams crackles onto a screen, one of the rare old black and white films of Hank performing. People munch on popcorn and greet one another in French, bound by the distinctions of their unique culture and a passion—that's the right word—for Hank.

Hugh Harris isn't the only "Hank" performing at the Liberty. Hank acts are lousy on the ground in Louisiana. Other musicians put on their essential white cowboy hats and their spin on the classics. But Hugh is the one who makes you believe you are back in time, witnessing a Hank Williams performance live. He's that good. Except for his height, he looks like Hank. Thin and handsome and mostly big hat. His polite, old-school manner—using the "Miss" and a woman's first name whenever he addresses her, for instance—add to his verisimilitude. Up close he might look too short or too old—he's in his thirties and claims an actor's prerogative to keep his height a secret—but once he begins to sing, you believe.

I've always been of two minds about Hank impersonators, imitators to the tenth power. On one hand, you think, what's the point? There will never be another Hank; a big hat does not Hank Williams make. I'd hate to see it get to the saturation point of Elvis imitators, cheapening the act simply by volume. I have been in Memphis in August for so-called "Dead Week." There are woman Elvises, black Elvises, Japanese Elvises, and hundreds of garden-issue, pork-chop-sideburns Elvises. I'd hate to see the Hank phenomenon take that kind of turn. So far it has not.

But, there have been Hank impersonators since the month he died, including Hank Jr., who was strapped into his pint-sized suit and act at Audrey's insistence. Even now a Hank grandson, Hank Jr.'s son Shelton, Hank Williams the Third, is doing his musical imitation in blue jeans, T-shirt and a hint of punk, for big audiences everywhere. Though he sounds like Hank, I can't stand the kid. He admits he "resorted" to the Hank act only because rock didn't pay the bills. "My father's never done crap for me in the music business," Shelton once told a reporter. That's not exactly true. Shelton was playing rock and installing garage doors until he realized the value of the family name. Only then did he switch to country—because he had to, he insisted. He sounds more like Hank than Bocephus does, but Shelton's is every bit as much an impersonator act as Hugh Harris's.

I don't have anything for Hank Jr., either, but he has helped that spoiled kid. Hank Jr. loaned his son one of the of the real Hank's shirts for a debut on the *Grand Ole Opry*. And in 1996 the two of them made an album and dubbed Shelton's grandfather's voice onto it: "Three Hanks: Men with Broken Hearts."

It always seemed to me that Jett Williams has more of a claim on a broken heart than two of those men. It took her years to establish her heritage, whereas the other two had it handed to 'em.

Hugh's is a far more humble presentation, if you will, which maybe is why it's better. A tribute act. A labor of love. It doesn't hurt that for years Don Helms, Hank's steel guitar player, was backing up all the various

Hanks in the Liberty show band, including Hugh's. Helms died in 2006. His sad licks were as much of the Hank signature, almost, as Hank's voice. Hank did a good day's work when he found Helms, no doubt about it.

Before meeting Hank, Don Helms had a little band that played around Montgomery. One day Hank walked into a music store and told the owner he needed a band. The owner pointed Hank in the direction of the pool hall, telling him to ask for Don Helms, who possibly could help. Hank hired Helms's band on the spot but then said: "Let's go to the pawn shop." Helms said it wouldn't be necessary; his band members all had their instruments. "It ain't for the instruments," Hank said. "It's for blackjacks. When you see the joints we play in, you'll understand why you need a blackjack."

If the story's not true, it ought to be.

BELIEVE IT OR NOT, Hugh has something Hank didn't have and few musicians anywhere have: a college degree in country music. Yes, Virgil, such a thing does exist, at Northeast Mississippi Junior College in Booneville, Mississippi. Long before I'd ever seen or heard of Hugh Harris, not all that long after he was born, I interviewed an old Booneville lawyer, Donald Franks, whose money helped make that academic choice possible. Franks was a lover of classic country, especially Hank, and wanted to insure its survival. So he donated a country curriculum to the little school in his hometown.

I was polite to Franks, of course, who was good to me and was a constant source of feature material over the years. He also raised miniature horses and knew where all the Booneville bodies were buried. But I remember thinking at the time, in an unfair and dismissive way, that country music should come from the school of hard knocks, not a junior college classroom. As Harlan Howard said of good country music, it's just "three chords and the truth." Having heard Hugh, I must revise my opinion. A little music theory won't kill your act. Won't make it, but won't necessarily hurt it, either.

Hugh Harris had to audition for his scholarship, and he sang an original song and Hank's "Your Cheatin' Heart." He won the financial help, and spent two years in Mississippi's Hill Country studying basic music theory, studio recording, history of country music, and keyboard piano and guitar.

Hugh is a smart man, a songwriter as well as a performer, who also works on historical fiction in his limited spare time. And because he's smart, he's thought about the man he imitates. He's tried to figure why Hank lasts and others don't. "The paradox of songwriting," he says, "of great, lasting, effective songwriting, is to write something that so uniquely applies to you that everyone can say, 'That applies especially to me.' No one was ever better at that than Hank Williams."

Hugh's day job in correction is something he doesn't talk about much. "I got into corrections just to help make a living, but I've stuck with it. At Angola I did a little bit of everything that you can do as an officer . . ."

After two years at infamous Angola prison farm he transferred to a much smaller corrections facility closer to his home, but Angola had to make a mighty impression. Anyone who has ever even visited the remote, eerily beautiful prison comes away changed. The place is 18,000 acres defined and kept naturally secure by the Mississippi River on three sides. There are more than 5,000 inmates and 1,800 men and women on staff. The worst offenders end up there, and over 70 percent are in for life and never leave. And though there's a Who's Who as long as your arm and bad as your worst nightmare, one of the most famous residents was a musician: Huddie William Ledbetter, known to posterity as Lead Belly. Billed by promoters late in his life as the "man who sang himself out of prison," not once but twice, Lead Belly's rendition of "Good Night Irene" can bring tears to the flintiest of eyes.

You'd either have to sing your way out or sprout wings to escape Angola. I've been there three times and, because I was on assignment, I've seen behind a few curtains. I was given an armed "escort" who let me talk to some of the prisoners but only the ones considered trusties. What strikes me every time I visit is how innocent all the prisoners appear when herded together in one place, like the annual prison rodeo. You might see just one of them on a corner and cross the street to avoid making eye contact. But, all together, there is a kind of boys' choir effect, as if *that many* men can't all have gone bad. Especially hard to distrust are the old men they corral together in one senior section for the rodeo. They look like grandfathers on a Sunday outing.

While Hank may have had a few run-ins with cops over shooting his pistols in the city limit, being drunk and disorderly, as far as I know he managed to avoid serious jail time despite numerous drunken escapades that put him on the wrong side of the law if not the bars. His short life was sentence enough. But something about Hugh's close encounters on a daily basis with men whose luck was sour and prospects nil had to inform his portrayal of Hank. You couldn't work there and not feel so lonesome you could cry.

I had to ask Hugh Harris the question. Hank was an old soul, looking much older than his twenty-nine years when he died. But what happens when Hugh slides inevitably into his forties, or fifties? Will he hang up his Hank hat? Park his boots in the back of some closet? "I have, generally, been blessed with a youthful appearance. I'll just see when the time comes that they don't 'see Hank' anymore when I'm up there, and I'll know . . ."

He may not be the best Hank act in the world. There's lots of competition. But for my money he has the best approach and manner. And Hugh has definitely settled in the best place to play Hank, and he knows it. "Hank liked his jokes, he liked his fun and . . . liked his spirits. I think that can be said about lots of us in south Louisiana . . ."

Some of us spend our lives looking for another Hank. Other fanatics may watch for UFO's, half expecting to be "taken up" when an errant satellite flashes in the sky or a cloud formation looks extraordinarily weird. My father watches, religiously, the cable show that features David Church and his regionally (the Midwest) famous Hank impersonation. It'll do in a pinch.

Chelsey, my niece, fell in love with Hank after she met the actor Jason Petty who portrayed Hank on Broadway. Petty was performing in the popular *Hank Williams: Lost Highway* at the Ryman when the Atlanta newspaper sent me to interview him. Chelsey rode along. I made her wear a dress.

Petty was thirty-two in 1997 when we met him, already in his second season playing Hank at the Ryman, packing the audience with geriatric bus groups and women wearing sequin and denim and men who looked a little like Travis Tritt if you squinted. Petty had learned country music from his grandmother, a widow who managed a tobacco farm forty miles from Nashville. Jason used to stand next to her in the Church of Christ, trying to match her soprano: "I'd grab a note and hold on."

For a while after college Jason sold advertising for a television station in Lexington, Kentucky. Soon he found work based in Nashville, a solid, two-state-territory job selling "facial implant system," whatever that was. But it is hard to stay the professional course in Nashville. There's that sweet, seductive music everywhere, streaming from orange cinder block lounges and open taxis and apartment windows. If you have the musical seed at all, it blooms in Nashville's hothouse of harmony. Jason surrendered. He got work for several seasons at *Opry*land, singing in a show called "Country Music U.S.A." He portrayed everyone from Elvis to Garth Brooks, displaying a real talent for musical impersonations. On days off he wrote his own songs, trying them out on small crowds at the Bluebird, the Broken Spoke, the Boardwalk. But then he got a break that most aspiring singer/songwriters wouldn't presume to dream. He got steady work as Hank.

"I'm a little awestruck walking around in his shoes on that stage," Jason said to Chelsey and me with commendable modesty. But it hadn't stopped him walking all the way to Off Broadway where no less than The New York Times declared in a headline: "Gone 50 Years, Hank Williams Is Back." Heady stuff. By the time we met he'd sang the "Lovesick Blues" for a thousand performances and was as cocksure as the real Hank.

But there was something even more memorable about the night than interviewing an actor/musician who nailed the part. It was the one time in my life I got to see a true conversion experience. That's what I remember the best. After meeting the young and handsome Petty at lunch, then hearing him sing Hank for a couple of hours on stage, Chelsey became a die-hard Hank fan. She immediately shook Jewel loose from her earphones and began playing Hank, all Hank, all the time. She memorized all the lyrics to his songs, and hated, as I often do, to hear modern renditions of his classics by other, trendier artists. Never would Chelsey make the mistakes I've heard other young people make, things like, "But Norah Jones wrote 'Cold, Cold Heart,' didn't she?" When her pre-teen friends all got the new country bug, Chelsey bravely stuck with the traditional. Once you've heard the best . . .

I, TOO, THOUGHT ANOTHER Hank might come along. I had great hopes, for instance, the first time I heard the voice of Randy Travis, who didn't write his own songs and whose name I now struggle to remember.

I think, and often, of the first time I heard my late husband Don sing. I would hear him sing thousands of times after that first night, sitting on the decks and porches and in the rooms that were part of our life together for sixteen years. But that first time it came as a shock. I had known him a while, and he had never even mentioned that he could sing.

It was late at night, and we were gypsies in the palace, if you will, temporarily using his brother's big house up the hill from Don's ragtag trailer. The brother was out of town. Don pulled his sibling's guitar off a hook on the wall and sat on a sofa and started casually strumming and asked what I wanted to hear. I said "Cold, Cold Heart" because that's what I always say when given the opportunity for a request. It's a test, really, like asking a blind date his opinion of capital punishment.

Don sang several verses, not in Hank's voice, but in a voice influenced by Hank, that harkened Hank, revered Hank, and knew something of the tribulation and sorrow that had gone into those words. Anyone who writes, and Don had written, realizes that without a certain depth of knowledge of the words you use, words are just words. Nothing more. And words without heft and depth do not last. They are as temporal as wild spring onions, sprouting but not mattering because what lies beneath the surface doesn't amount to much.

Hank was dead, and Don would die far too soon, but something about Don's rendition of that song that night made everything bearable, makes everything bearable now. The song is evidence that you are not alone, no matter how lonely. Others have bravely gone where you are going, have come out the other end and made art along the way. That's one thing you never hear about Hank, but something I've often thought. He was brave. He was in pain most of his life, but he soldiered on. He was negotiating a commercial labyrinth infamous for stiffing "the talent." His personal life was defined by a free-spending, ambitious wife and a domineering mother. Or, as Billie Jean would say when interviewed on a documentary about Hank's life: "Hank was tied up with some bitches."

It's hard in this life to recognize your true talents, to stick to task, to let all the rest go. Hank knew how to do that, spent his short time alive making hay.

The night Don sang Hank, I was blown away.

CHAPTER TEN

"Ninety-nine percent of the world's lovers are not with their first choice. That's what makes the jukebox play."

— WILLIE NELSON

In the early 1980s, as a young reporter, it fell my lot to cover a B. B. King concert in the dusty rodeo arena of Parchman Prison farm in Sunflower County, Mississippi. As assignments go, this was choice. Not only did you get to hear the legendary bluesman riff away on his best gal Lucille, you got to stand in the blinding heat of a Delta day, enjoying the nervousness of the burly armed guards who instinctively put their hands over their guns whenever B. B. belted out one about freedom.

If you're doing thirty to life at Parchman, you can't hear "Chains and Things" and not take it personally, and the guards had that much sense. As Robbie Robertson has said, "Music should never be harmless."

We reporters, amazingly only three or four of us, were situated in the dead center of the arena, standing directly in front of the stage, no chairs, even, on which to prop. If this had been a real rodeo, we'd have been the clowns. I looked around and quietly planned my exit route in case of a riot. I think everyone there expected something to boil over.

As concerts go, it was amazingly electric. And I don't just mean the guitar. The music was release for men who really needed it. It was a musical mockery of the walls and halls that held them, the guns that trained on them day and night. Music can lift you up, and out.

Nothing bad happened that hot day, no riots or shootings. The music was enough, that day, for those men. I'd have to say, all in all, considering the edgy setting and the superb blues, B. B. King at Parchman was my next-to-favorite concert ever. It was music to give flight by. I'll tell you about my favorite concert later, at the end of this book. If I finish it.

I was, at the time of the Parchman concert, living in a one-room apartment in Greenville, Mississippi, working for the Memphis newspaper, and Parchman Prison was the best part of my beat. The Delta to me was magical, one long crop row of a region, flat and dark as a heart-pine floor. I never wanted for good stories. Not in the Delta, land of drama. And native son B. B. King's music fit that day and place the way the baby fits grandma's lap. He gave comfort and solace to men who are most often forgotten.

Before the concert, B. B. graciously met with a few of us, laughing and answering our rather timid and formal questions. "How did Lucille get her name?" At a juke joint in Twist, Arkansas, a fire was started when two denizens knocked over the kerosene-filled barrel that sat in the middle of the room and heated the place. The men were fighting over a woman named Lucille. B. B. King foolishly rushed back into the burning building when he realized he'd left his $30 guitar inside. Two men died in the fire. B. B. said he named that guitar (and all others since) Lucille to remember never again to act that impulsively—or fight over women.

B. B. seemed to be enjoying himself, despite the repetitive, endless questions. I can see him now, lounging with feet up, a big, brown, leather recliner of a man. He was only in his mid-fifties then, but his expressive bronze face held the wisdom of the ages. We all sat in the official visitors' quarters just inside Parchman's front gate. But it might have been Buckingham Palace instead of Parchman. He was royalty. And if "laid-back" has a poster child, it's B. B.

In 1984, I would be in the same building for a far different reason. I was there to report, with others, the execution of child-murderer Jimmy Lee Gray. Mississippi cranked up its gas chamber for the first time in nineteen years that night, and it was hell to sit and wait for the state to take a life. Capital punishment protestors were marching just outside the gate, futilely raising objections and candles into a starlit Delta night, while inside we all paced and nervously chatted, marking time, forgetting to use the infamous gallows humor reporters are famous for, waiting to hear that the grim business was over, that the state was satisfied. An eye for an eye and all that.

It was the only really unpleasant time I ever had at Parchman, believe it or not. I've decided I have an affinity for prisons. Usually the stories I filed were about federal court-ordered changes that made life marginally better for those spending their days and nights on the eighteen thousand acres of Mississippi River Valley-rich land with piss-poor prospects. I didn't ever mind going to Parchman. Something about knowing you could drive back out that gate made going in tolerable, even exciting. But the night Jimmy Lee Gray died was not exciting, or even perversely interesting, as I'd expected it might be. It was horrible.

That awful night I didn't "win" the reporters' lottery to be an official witness for the rest of the reporters' pool, a dubious honor if ever there was one. The night they gassed Jimmy Lee, thank god, some other reporters got "lucky." And those who did attend as witnesses soon came back with a genuine horror story. As he was gassed, Gray's head had banged again and again against a steel pole situated behind the chamber's chair, rendering the punishment problematically cruel and certainly unusual.

"While prison and attending medical officials insisted that the violent head banging did not matter because Gray was clinically dead, the damage had been done," Donald A. Cabana wrote in an article for the Mississippi Historical Society. The next year the legislature enacted a law replacing the gas chamber with lethal injection.

But on the summer's day when I met B. B. King, the inmates were jubilant, running the asylum, in spirit, anyhow. It was as if everyone there got a couple of hours' reprieve. Here was a great artist, a commercial success, a black man from Indianola, just down the road in the same county, who, but for the grace of Lucille, might have been stuck here at Parchman. Poverty and race certainly can put you there. Instead, the bluesman was an honored guest, the Man in Charge, the toast of the rodeo arena. The irony wasn't lost on any of us—prisoners, guards, visitors. There's such a fine line between doing time and keeping time that honest folks have to admit there's a degree of luck involved in staying outside the fence. Maybe that's why so many musicians have addressed the grim reality of jails, prisons, even daybreak executions. Country songs, in particular, are full of sad old padres, branded ex-cons, and men with broken hearts.

That concert I was paid to attend. But for another, by the great Bob Dylan, I saved up for months to buy a ticket. I was making reporter's wages in Alabama, and discretionary income was nonexistent. I loved Dylan, though I'd come to him rather late, embracing protest music only after the 1960s were past. The times essentially had changed before I realized they needed to. The joke was that the Sixties didn't get to Auburn till the Seventies. And I wasn't even the first wave ashore musically at Auburn.

The Dylan concert was staged in a huge, boring convention hall in Birmingham. I wore a new green wool skirt and sweater and boots that I bought on credit at the Jewish-owned clothing store in Lanett, Alabama. Why I dressed like a Mississippi Sunday School teacher to attend a Dylan concert befuddles my memory now. Our seats were so bad that Little Bobby Zimmerman definitely still looked little. He was late to appear. A late arrival was de rigueur for most stars at all rock concerts. When finally he showed, Dylan played his standards, but an eerie electrified version of what had been acoustic hits. I was dreadfully disappointed. It would have been like paying to see Hank Williams sing punk.

Bob Dylan always has said Hank Williams influenced him more than any other singer. "I started writing songs after I heard Hank Williams," he said on a 1965 television show. That Birmingham concert day, however, Dylan forgot his roots. I felt better about the whole thing recently when Jett Williams told me her niece, Hilary Williams, Bocephus's daughter and also a singer, said to her one day: "I saw Bob, and he asked about you." The always-humble Jett was puzzled. "Bob who?"

When it's Dylan, you can forgive an off night. His description of Hank's death alone is a poem: "Kept my fingers crossed, hoped it wasn't true. But it was true. It was like a great tree had fallen. Hearing about Hank's death caught me squarely on the shoulder. The silence of outer space never seemed so loud."

The only thing worse in live concerts I witnessed came decades later. I was, finally, seeing Jerry Lee Lewis in person, in Tupelo, only to be surrounded by a geriatric crowd that didn't clap or boogie or do any of the things that Jerry Lee makes you want to do when you're listening to him alone, at home. It was the biggest collection of prigs I've ever been in the midst of, and I've covered the taping of a Jim and Tammy Faye Bakker television show.

Nobody moved, or clapped, or sang along, much less engaged in the salacities you envision when you hear Jerry Lee. I've danced in my socks and underwear to "Great Balls of Fire" more times than I'd like to admit, and it's damn hard to sit still when Jerry Lee cranks it up. Anyone sane would agree. But somehow these fans managed. I had always wanted to hear the Killer live, but not if the crowd was dead.

I self-consciously tried to start a chain reaction, a wiggle and a wave of movement, but all I got were dirty looks. Jerry Lee himself was in fine form. He didn't seem to notice that the fans were comatose. I think that Jerry Lee, like B. B., was so caught up in his own music that he didn't need response. Should have saved my money on that one and hoped to catch Jerry Lee in the small nightclub he frequents around Memphis.

Mostly I've been lucky in live concerts that were lively. Willie Nelson, in particular, always gives you your money's worth. His band may take a break, but not Willie. While the boys go behind the curtain to rest and smoke and joke, Willie soldiers on alone, playing that old holey, and holy, guitar of his and acting just like it's the first time he ever sang whatever song he's singing. You half expect to see a master of ceremonies appear with a hook to pull him off the stage so an aging audience exhausted from affirming Willie can go home and get to bed; that's how much he loves performing.

There was a legendary Hank performance, near his end, at the Skyline Club in Austin, Texas. Hank had been so ill on the road that his handlers called Lilly and had her flown out to help. "Normally, Hank would have performed a forty-five-minute medley that would lead to the intermission," biographer Paul Hemphill wrote. "But there would be no intermission this night. Once he strolled onto the stage and bent over the microphone, strumming his guitar, weaving like a cobra, they couldn't get him off. He sang every song he knew—more than once, if the bellowing crowd wanted it—going for three solid hours without a break . . ."

Maybe Hank knew he owed his fans something for all the missed shows and sloppy, drunken renditions. And he tried to pay it all back in one night.

Kris Kristofferson has a song on his wise, silver-threaded album, "Final Attraction." *They love you so badly for sharing their sorrows. . . Go break a heart.*

Guess it's not so easy, night after night, breaking hearts for others.

Linda Ronstadt's voice has no rival. But in concert in Jackson, Mississippi, she looked bored out of her skull. She played through the entire set without introducing a song or the band or making small talk of any kind. I'd always admired her as much for her outlook as her voice. She once told a magazine interviewer that she never wanted adult clothes. The photos that went with the article showed Linda barefoot and in cutoffs, walking in the surf. So I guess I expected a maverick like Linda Ronstadt to want a connection with a cheering audience.

Another disappointment registered. But maybe she was tired of sharing our sorrows, shouldering our unfulfilled desires to be mavericks, too.

Willie Nelson, on the other hand, never looks bored, never looks to be living beyond the moment. It is part of his mystique, and perhaps what he learned from Hank's better performances: Play it like it's the first time.

"I always thought Hank Williams was a great person to listen to . . . because his messages were simple, to the point, usually just three chords but they hit you right in the bone," Willie has said.

The theories are endless about the Hank/audience connection. Why was Hank's heart so much more accessible to the people who paid to hear him than any other performer, pop or country? Sixty years later, why do people remember his performances the way they talk about the night when man first walked on the moon?

"He was great with his audiences because he figured they were like himself," Boots Harris told the Griersons. "He didn't talk down to them, or up. Hank just looked in the mirror."

"He had a lot of confidence," Chet Atkins said. "He was always singing a song he had written. He used to point to Audrey and say, 'There's my song barometer. I sing all my songs for her. If she like them, the public will like them.'"

"I think the most interesting thing about Hank Williams was his eyes," Minnie Pearl told the Griersons. "He had dark, mysterious, unfathomable eyes . . ."

The audiences recognized authenticity. Hank was bona fide. He was real. As Charlie Parker once said, "If you don't live it, it won't come out of your horn."

Hank had lived it, loved it, plowed it, drunk it. And his audiences instinctively trusted his take on a life not so unlike their own.

Irene Hall, the widow of a Nashville pipefitter, told the Griersons she once was on her way to Baton Rouge where her husband was seeking employment when they heard Hank Williams perform at Shreveport on the *Louisiana Hayride*. "Johnny Horton introduced him. You could hear a pin drop . . . He sang the song 'Lovesick Blues.' He sang about three or four lines, and the audience just went wild. Red Sovine was also on the program, but when Hank got through singing, everybody left, even though the show wasn't over. We didn't care about hearing the rest of them."

We didn't care about hearing the rest of them. Strong testimonial.

"His popularity and enduring iconic status is due to his ability to capture the emotions, hopes, fears and heartbreaks of all of us," Jett Williams said. "When I go overseas performing, I say everybody's heart breaks the same, whether you are in Germany, Japan, or Opp, Alabama."

Hank's still the doctor to call.

I WAS IN MY fifties before I ever saw the *Grand Ole Opry*, though I'd been to the Mother Church, the Ryman, for a tour and for other concerts. I always figured the *Opry* might be redundant; I'd heard those singers and their songs all my life, quite literally. But, thank goodness, Don insisted. And he didn't insist on much. We would go to the *Opry*, by god, and if there were acts we didn't like, well, none of them lasted over ten minutes. I agreed and off we went.

As usual, Don was right. There was just something about being in that venerable place. About hearing, up close and in person, all of those Jeannies—Jeannie Seely, Jeanne Pruett, Jean Shepard. About seeing Little Jimmy Dickens strutting about, engulfed by his big cowboy hat. About watching the square dancers clog in their anachronistic shirtwaists. It was *important* somehow to witness the consummate showman Porter Wagoner open his coat to display a secret, sequined message—*Howdy!*—just one of the many cornball touches in a show that still played to us hicks from the Deep South and Midwest and hamlets everywhere. More corn than in all of Iowa, that's what the *Opry* is made of. It's cool because it's definitely not trying to be. I loved it and quickly bought tickets twice, three times, again.

It was as if I'd been there every Saturday night of my life, clapping and hee-hawing, waiting with limited patience for the most important *Opry* act to appear. Surely he is in the wings, having a snort, joshing with other musicians, flirting with the women, waiting for a man with a clipboard to tell him he's up next. For the overriding thought at the Ryman, no matter who is performing or what's being sung, is Hank, that he was here, hell, that he *is* here. There's the rudimentary peace from the knowledge that Hank owned that stage from the moment he stepped foot on it. Here, finally, is something tangible left of the flash of white light that was Hank. You almost feel sorry for all the others who presume to stand there and sing where he once stood. The *Opry* might fire him for drunkenness and missed appearances, he might leave this vale of tears, but still Hank remains the star. He's dead, but it's his stage, his crowd, his music. Nobody yet has wrested it away. What majestic irony. Damn. He did get out of this world alive.

One could even make the argument that it's Hank we've all come to see, not the others at all. The rest are supporting cast. Bit players. And if we've arrived a few decades too late, it's better than nothing, inhabiting for a time this Camelot with its King Arthur missing.

I've made pilgrimages to Hank's grave off and on since I was seven years old. It's become one of my few traditions, plugging an azalea branch into a Jack or Old Granddad bottle and leaving it on the grave. It's as if the visit to Hank's grave takes care of all my cemetery visits for the year; once you've paid homage to the man who sang all our stories, you've taken care of business. I've been there alone only once. I've arrived alone many times, but always, always, someone else is paying his respects. You don't even have to exchange pleasantries; you are floating in the same bottle of formaldehyde.

But going to the Ryman is different. At the graveyard, Hank is dead. A mortal just like the rest of us, powerless in the same ways we all will be powerless eventually. His ex-wife is at his side through eternity whether he wanted her there or not. That's a real lack of control.

At the Ryman, on the other hand, Hank comes alive. He is resurrected. And not so much by the music, though certainly there's that, or the mention of his name, which happens a lot. Not by the countless geegaws you can buy that carry his image.

Hank comes alive, starts to stir, because we've been carrying him around in our heads and hearts all these years, and finally, finally, we have a proper place to put him.

CHAPTER ELEVEN

"He was a friend of mine . . ."

— BOB DYLAN

Braxton Schuffert, at ninety-five, still has a showman's demeanor and presence, an enviable sixth sense about what to wear and say to impress an audience, albeit a small one this day.

We meet in his home, his "mansion on the hill," as he calls it, in Prattville, Alabama, a bustling Montgomery suburb. He bought the cozy, conventional home for his late wife, Ola Frances Till, who died suddenly and too young while sitting with her devoted husband at their kitchen table. She had been on the telephone moments before, then suddenly slumped over, dead. He demonstrates the scene. It was a moment so sad that he's been sentenced to relive it again and again.

But Braxton Schuffert is, for the most part, an upbeat, personable, funny man. He has a confident air. Both of us are eager for what I've come to think of as "Hank talk," as much about paying homage as gleaning information. I am armed with notebook and questions, Brack—"My friends call me Brack"—with his stories. He's wearing an ornately-stitched western shirt, a bolo tie with Hank's familiar face, and a smile the size of a container car. He is tall, dark, and still handsome; he could pass for eighty-five, even eighty. Once a singing cowboy, always a singing cowboy.

If there could be a mirror-image story to that of our hero Hank Williams, Braxton Schuffert lived it, is living it. Both men were good pickers and singers, believers, native Alabamians, and friends as close as brothers. But at some point their lives split apart. One became the photographic negative, the other the print.

Braxton Schuffert, at Miss Lillian's behest, helped Hank start his first band when Hank was only fifteen and Brack was a wise and worldly twenty-one. The band had a modest start, playing for Montgomery's firemen and policemen on their respective pay days, at sweet-sixteen birthday parties, marathon dances, and eventually blue highway honkytonks. From those beginnings, Hank Williams spun off into fame, fortune, familial upheaval, heavy drink, early death, and legend.

"By the end, Hank had to go on a drunk to get a vacation," Brack says, and regret is palpable when he says it. Not a judgment, an observation.

Brack, on the other hand, *kept his hand upon the throttle,* as the old hymn admonishes, turning down a chance at a life on the road and *Opry* stardom, driving a delivery truck, working four decades for the same meat company, living a quiet family life, burying and mourning his wife of many years, taking pride in his grandchildren. Today, this day, Brack Schuffert sits in the one place his friend Hank will never be: content in his twilight years, reminiscing at his kitchen table.

A man of order, Brack keeps his house as neat as the proverbial pin. The floor is mopped. The nice mahogany dining room suite he bought for his wife is still adorned with silk flowers. An old-fashioned percolator is on the stove, on the ready. He does the housekeeping himself. Characteristically for a man of such order, he likes to start at the beginning of a story, and, for Brack, the beginning of his most important story is the day he met Hank.

It was, he says, at Miss Lillian's Montgomery boarding house, not on a downtown street outside a radio station—the way one of Hank's biographers described it. At the time, Brack was driving a Hormel Meat Packing Company truck which made routine deliveries to the boarding house. One day, as he delivered Miss Lillian's order, he noticed a boy-sized guitar, a Gibson, lying on the living room sofa. Drawn to it like a bee to nandina, Brack picked up the guitar and played and sang two or three songs.

I got a girl on the Mobile Road / Makes more money than Henry Ford . . .

A seasoned performer already—he had starred on a show on two local radio stations for five years as "the Singing Cowboy"—Braxton Schuffert had plenty of songs to sing at the drop of a hat. Many of the songs he had written.

"Come here, Hiram," Miss Lillian called out to her son listening from another room. "He's got you beat."

Lilly knew her boy. Young Hiram emerged from wherever he'd been hiding, took his guitar, and started singing. Hank Williams didn't ever like being beat. Not in the singing department.

Brack was so impressed with the mature voice that came from the tall, skinny young boy that he invited Hank to ride with him the next day. "I said to Hank, 'I'm going to deliver the CC camps (Civilian Conservation Corps) in Troy and Andalusia tomorrow, and I'm leaving at daylight.'"

Next day, around 6 o'clock, Hiram was ready, standing outside that boarding house waiting for Brack.

All day long they rode and sang, Brack introducing his young friend to those who asked along the route as "my little brother." Men bond in the strangest ways, and the spontaneous hootenanny in the cab of that truck as it rolled through Alabama hill and dale did the trick. For the rest of his short life, Hank would call Brack when he needed to talk to someone he could trust, someone who never hit him up for money or favors, someone who encouraged but never judged. For his part, Hank constantly tried to thank Brack for being such a friend. He wrote songs for Brack, got him an MGM recording session and thus the opportunity to join the pantheon of country music singers: the *Grand Ole Opry*.

Perhaps the greatest testament to what Hank felt for his older friend, his "big brother": Brack never once saw Hank drunk. Saw him drinking, but never drunk.

Hank wasn't writing his own songs when they first met, though, and only knew a dozen old ones, certainly not all the current hits that Brack played on his radio shows. But the boy was a musical sponge, and he absorbed everything quickly as the newly minted singing duo rode in that Hormel meat truck all the way to Birmingham, a city Hank had never seen. "Hank was smart," Brack says.

That ride was, to use an old movie line, the beginning of a beautiful friendship.

MISS LILLIAN, NEVER ONE to ignore an opportunity, saw the influence Brack wielded over the boy, and decided it was good. Brack was the youngest of thirteen siblings from Shelby County. "By the time they got to me, they'd run out of names and looks, too," he jokes. Coming from that large, poor family, his work ethic had been established early, and forever. He'd seen his sisters going to work in a cotton mill, and his brother working on the railroad. They were a can-do family of workers, and Brack, the baby, was no exception. The Schuffert clan migrated to Montgomery when Brack was a small boy. By the time he was ten he was throwing the *Montgomery Advertiser* on a large downtown paper route, ". . . and I could knock the door down."

The clean-cut, hard-working Brack was the perfect older brother figure for Hank who, for all purposes, had grown up fatherless. Miss Lillian encouraged the friendship and the start-up of a new band by ordering blue Western shirts, boots, hats, and bandanas from a company in Carlsbad, New Mexico. "We just wore our own pants," Brack explains. He still has the cowboy hat, which threatened to disintegrate the last time he wore it. It is on loan now to the Hank Williams Museum.

"Everybody says Mrs. Williams was so mean," Brack muses. "She was sweet to me. And she worked hard to feed a lot of musicians . . ." Tough, hard-working, perhaps too invested in Hank's talent. But certainly not mean, he says.

Playing alongside Hank and Brack in the new band was Smith "Hezzy" Adair, an orphan who had come from the streets to live for a couple of years with Brack and his mother. Brack had met Hezzy one day when leaving the radio station, had heard the youngster playing harmonica, "choking every note," as Brack puts it. After Hank Williams entered the picture, Hezzy soon moved to the boarding house—where the action was. "Hezzy and Hank got to be big buddies out of that bottle, you know," Brack says.

Hezzy also played bass. The obligatory fiddle player—every country band at the time had one—was Freddy Beach, who was left-handed but couldn't afford to buy a left-handed fiddle so simply played his father's, tuned for a right-handed fiddler. Hank's sister Irene was a vocalist and at times took up tickets, and, of course, Hank and Brack played guitar and sang. In his unselfish fashion, Brack, already a fixture on the Alabama music scene, soon stepped back and let the more ambitious Hank sing lead. It was deference Hank never forgot. He spent the rest of his life trying to repay Brack.

"I didn't give him his voice or his ability to write, but I got him going," Brack says. He's not bragging, just stating fact. And it just might be as significant a contribution to the arts as Boswell made for Johnson. The fellows even traveled to their first gigs in Brack's car, necessarily, since he was the only one in the band who owned a car. Miss Lillian had yet to buy her first automobile.

The Drifting Cowboys in subsequent years would morph more frequently than a Michael Jackson video. But this was the first assembly. And as the first, it was important, even historic. This incarnation of Hank's Drifting Cowboys was Hank's first taste of impressing the home folks, his kin, the girls. And he liked it. They played Hank's hometown for their first major show, giving Hank a chance to show old neighbors and relatives what he was about now. There were shows scheduled at Georgiana High School and several other sites in Butler County.

Brack and Hank couldn't resist stopping, between engagements, by the Baptist church to impress the girls with their cowboy outfits. Works every time. That night they walked two young ladies home from church, sitting on the front porch and holding hands until, startlingly, an electric light came on. Electric lights in rural Alabama remained an oddity then, and Hank and Brack were unlucky enough that night to roost beneath one.

They spent the rest of that night at Hank's Uncle Ed Skipper's, sleeping together on the spare bed, so exhausted by their glorious debut that the biscuits were cold when finally they rose the next morning.

In a way they were like Army buddies, joined at the hip, a friendship forged in the trenches. Some of those backroad juke joints could seem like combat zones, with male patrons who weren't shy about picking fights with band members who inevitably attracted *their* women. When Braxton really did go into the army during World War II, Hank's band carried on without him. The army didn't want Hank with his bad back. Hank tried to join, but even a wartime army rejected him. Then he tried welding at a defense plant in Mobile. That didn't last long either, though how that professional tangent ended depends on whom you ask. Some say Miss Lillian went and fetched her son home. It doesn't much matter. The bottom line is that Hank kept singing, and began some serious song-writing, the part of the business he preferred over all else.

Meanwhile, Brack was enduring thirty-mile arbitrary hikes in the heat of Abilene, Texas, with a rock in his mouth for moisture, swearing to himself that if ever he got home he'd nail his feet to the ground. Chosen for Leadership School, Brack was reluctant to "lead." But he acquitted himself well in the service and never was shipped overseas. Still, the *idea* of not returning hung like a threat over him. And it made him vow to be a good family man if ever he did make it home.

So World War II forged both men, in a way, but differently. It made Braxton a determined homebody, grateful to get out of the service in one piece and to get back between the traces and stay there. And it showed Hank, already an outsider, that music was not only his passion but his best bet at a livelihood. It was something he could do with a bad back, and do well. Their paths were set. And they had diverged. But the friendship never wavered. It lasted. Until the bittersweet end.

The last two weeks of his life an exhausted, depressed and seriously ill Hank spent his Christmas break mostly in the bed at Miss Lillian's. A country music superstar, at the young age of twenty-nine Hank was spent. Brack saw him nearly every day those two weeks. He still regrets not driving Hank to that infamous New Year's show that never was in Canton, Ohio. Brack thinks he might could have made a difference, might have known Hank well enough to see he needed a hospital, not a pretend doctor handing out choral hydrate like leftover Christmas candy. It was, in fact, that sad December 1952 when Hank entreated Braxton Schuffert for the last time to go with him on the road.

One last time, Braxton said, "No."

They had had the same discussion over and over. Hank begging Brack to go on the road and play music. Brack saying, no, he'd better keep the dependable Hormel job that he knew would pay his family's bills. Hank would call from Nashville. "You're as good as anybody up here," Hank would coax.

One day, Hank made an end run around the dutiful Brack and called his wife at the bank where she worked. Hank told her he'd arranged for an MGM recording session for Brack on a Monday morning, and that her husband should catch the train to Nashville where Hank would pick him up at the station. He'd be staying at the Hermitage Hotel. Brack was human, after all, and he thought, "Why not?"

His boss at Hormel told Brack he could have the time off to go to Nashville to make a record if he found a substitute salesman. He'd been promoted from truck driver by then. So the conscientious Brack made out a route sheet for the substitute, took a Monday and Tuesday off and got on a train bound for Nashville.

It was at Hank's Nashville home on Franklin Road in a paneled den Audrey called the "Music Room" that Brack first met Fred Rose. Rose, who was all business, was there to plan the next day's recording session. He said one song would be Johnny Wright's "If Tears Would Bring You Back" and another Hank's "Why Should I Cry?" That left two more songs to fill the two-record session.

Hank picked up his Martin and strummed "a new one," something he was calling "A Teardrop on a Rose." He sang it, then gave it to Brack, the way a bride tosses a bridesmaid her bouquet. It was a beautiful thing—both the song and the gesture.

The last song for the session Brack and Hank wrote together, a ditty called "Rockin' Chair Daddy," which took about fifteen minutes and was inspired by Brack's comment: "I'm not lazy, just tired." Fred Rose gave the song his blessing but, demonstrating his famed and uncanny ability to tweak a song, instructed Brack to "sing it a little higher there at the end."

The next day, backed by the most famous version of the Drifting Cowboys and using Hank's guitar, Brack made his two records. Rose suggested that the name "Schuffert" would be too hard to pronounce, casually changing the spelling to "Shooford."

The "Teardrop" song became wildly popular, and the *Opry*, encouraged by Brack's famous friend Hank, beckoned. Hank phoned to report as much, telling Brack he needed to quit Hormel and hie to Nashville. This was the *Grand Ole Opry*, for god's sake. Brack refused. "I told the good Lord if he got me home safe from the Army, I'd stay there."

A recording star who wouldn't hit the road to promote his music was of no use to a dog-eat-dog industry based on tours and travel and constant exposure. You struck while the iron was hot. You went out to your fans, they didn't come to you. Braxton Schuffert was turning his back on a life many desperately wanted, still want, but one not conducive to family. And family was his first priority. Or, as Brack says:

"After that, the Singing Cowboy went to sleep for thirty years."

BRAXTON SCHUFFERT WAS A pallbearer, of course. Along with Fred and Wesley Rose, Brack helped move that dreadful coffin up the steep steps of the city auditorium, into and out again. The night before the funeral, when they took Hank's casket home to Miss Lillian's, he stood over his friend's body till 10 or 11 o'clock when Lon Williams, Hank's father, arrived. "He was a good man, Lon. He was a Mason. That says it all."

"'I want to get flowers for my son's grave,'" Brack said Lon told him. Brack protested because of the hour, but soon the two man were rapping on the door of a local florist's home at Rosemont Gardens.

"I knocked with my pocket knife," Brack recalls. When he told the florist who was with him—"It's Hank Williams's father and he wants flowers for his son"—despite the hour, the door opened.

"I'm a poor man," Lon told the florist. "All I have to spend is $5."

Five dollars bought a lot of flowers when the deceased was Hank Williams. "His father walked away from there with all the flowers he could carry."

After Braxton tells me the funeral story, he gets his mint-condition 1948 Martin guitar with its red strap from the case and gives me a private concert. He starts out sitting, but soon enough pushes back from the kitchen table and declares: "You can't sit down and get it out!" Sure enough, his still-strong voice gets a boost that you hadn't realized it needed. More Ray Price than Hank Williams, he sings "Glory Bound

Train" with its wonderful train noises, and "Mary," a song about his sister, both original creations.

All he writes now are gospel songs, and his own vocal range isn't really conducive to singing many of Hank's. For a while he would not sing his friend Hank's songs at all. A religious conversion seemed to him to prohibit that. Now, well, he makes exceptions.

The Singing Cowboy has outlasted many of the Drifting Cowboys, including the more famous ones like fiddler Jerry Rivers and steel guitarist Don Helms. Not long ago Brack strapped on his old guitar to sing a benefit concert for the local museum. Tornado sirens were screaming during part of his performance, but he carried on.

Braxton recently has been honored by the Alabama Legislature for his contribution to the arts, and he is active in his church where once a month a fellowship called NDY—Not Dead Yet—gathers for potluck and music. He still is a cowboy, the real kind, with a cattle farm outside town that he regularly visits. It's hard now to argue with the lifestyle choice he made so long ago, to keep delivering and selling bacon and Spam, sticking close to family and home and routine, instead of chasing fame and fortune on that relentless road.

It's not in his character to dwell on what might have been.

CHAPTER TWELVE

"When my bed gets empty, I get to feelin' kind
of mean and blue. The springs are getting' rusty,
sleepin' single like I do . . ."

— BESSIE SMITH, "EMPTY BED BLUES"

My small apartment in Greenville in the Mississippi Delta was at the intersection of Eureka and Star streets in a bedraggled, funky part of that old river town. There was a little Chinese grocery nearby called, aptly enough, The Star-Reka, where many nights I'd stop to pick up delicious fried rice to take home for supper. The Chinese butcher there was known for his whimsical meat case, replete with meat sculptures —raw and red ground beef shaped like a cow one week, pork sculpted into a convincing pig the next. Having grown up a butcher's daughter, I have and always had a true and abiding appreciation for meat; I just never realized till then you could treat it as *art*. The Chinese population in the Delta was significant, mostly the descendants of laborers brought in to build the levee that kept the Mississippi River at bay. You were never going to starve to death in Greenville if you had a couple of dollars for the Chinese take-out available at every 7-Eleven and Pit Stop.

My one-room apartment was a long and narrow addition across the back of an old home that belonged to a sweet and pleasingly dramatic widow who taught music. Mary Manning taught organ, enthusiastically, and some nights I'd be awakened by a spirited rendition of "Lady of Spain" or "Fur Elise." I always expected the wee-hour concerts coincided with the days when a doctor made house calls and gave Miss Manning vitamin shots and an admirable rush of energy.

In what was for me a fortunate coincidence, she loved newspaper reporters and the extra income from the modest rent she charged a series of us who worked in a tiny bureau office for the Memphis's *Commercial Appeal.* Before me, another bureau reporter named David had occupied the one-room rental, and David, as A. J. Liebling once wrote of Earl Long, could charm the socks off a rooster. He was not only personable, but talented and young. He loved both the reporting life and high fashion, making his regular rounds to the federal courthouse in town and the sheriff's office in get-ups my grandfather would have called fitting for a "dirt-road sport." David and I got to know one another pretty well in the two-week overlap the newspaper insisted on so the veteran bureau person could show "new meat" the ropes. I lived in a run-down motel for that short period, waiting to inherit Miss Manning's apartment. It would seem like a mansion after the motel room. I think I may have been the third or fourth bureau person to rent it.

Though older and more seasoned, I was impressed by David's aggressive reporting style. He had the zest for the reporting end of the game, while I much preferred the writing. If I live to be a hundred I won't forget covering the sentencing phase of a murder trial in Yazoo City during our tandem ride in the Greenville news bureau. We were a team. I was to write the news story; he was to provide "the art." For every published black and white photograph a bureau reporter contributed, we got an extra five dollars. That meant a lot to most of us. To that end, David lurked in the back courthouse corridors, hoping to snap a photograph of the murderer as he left the courtroom. When the black hat was taken out an unexpected way, David, small in stature, wrapped one skinny leg around a banister and swung precariously into thin air to get the faraway shot. He earned his five dollars.

David's goal in life was to be called into the "Big House," the Memphis newsroom, which is what all of us in the bureaus wanted. But that promotion wasn't happening fast enough to suit his ambitious nature. So he was leaving in a semi-huff for another newspaper job in another state, while owing money to everyone in the Mississippi Delta town. Especially the clothing stores, where he'd shopped for flamboyant shirts, hats, and footwear. He seemed to believe a reporter should dress like a cross between Philip Marlowe and Shaft.

For months after David's departure, Miss Manning kept getting his late notices from clothing stores and shoe shops and jewelers. But she never seemed to hold that against her friend and often asked if I heard from him.

I never did. Not until one day when word spread like intestinal flu between Memphis reporters, the credible gossip that David had been fired from his new job—in Texas, I believe—for manufacturing quotes. After that, every good story—and he'd written more than a few—became suspect. By violating the most scared of all journalistic tenets, he had undone his own work, erased every clever phrase he'd come up with, deleted it as if it had never been written. Word was he had asked on his proverbial knees to return to the *Commercial Appeal*, but the newspaper couldn't, wouldn't touch him. I think it pained the tri-state editor, who was a fair and sensitive man. But a newspaper cannot afford a tainted reporter.

Not too long afterwards, David, that dazzling dandy and crackerjack of a reporter, took his own life. Mary Manning cried when I told her.

I SOMETIMES THINK ABOUT David when I get the blues. He was so young, so very young when he ended it for himself. I guess there are some hurts even music can't reach.

It occurs to me as I write these words that I'm only about ten years younger now than Miss Manning was then. In that condescending way of the young, I sometimes felt extremely sorry for her, sensing her loneliness. I also thought she was for the most part wasting her time when, at her insistence, we'd go together to the Holiday Inn lounge and troll for possible suitors—for her, I was married. But I also was forty years younger than Miss Manning, and in my prime, looks-wise. We played a kind of cruel bait-and-switch, with both of us ordering a beer and appearing to settle in for some serious partying in that dark, musky lounge. When inevitably some lonely salesman would buy us both drinks, I would take a few sips and excuse myself, never to return.

Greenville was a fascinating place, the birthplace of such different personalities as puppeteer Jim Henson, author Shelby Foote, and Mary Wilson of the Supremes. I never had to search far for ideas for feature stories, and the federal courthouse filled my daily news quota when everything else was quiet.

All of this happened in 1980, before everybody with a D battery had portable boom boxes and IPods and computers, traveling music that could move right along with them. My stereo system at home, in Jackson, Mississippi, where Jimmy continued to live and work, had speakers the size of two wooden infant coffins. A stereo then was not something you moved about, not to a temporary residence, which is what I had. So I was, for the first time in my life, without music. My car had only an AM radio. Except for the organ that shook the house at the oddest of hours, there was an unaccustomed silence in my life. I might have invested in a radio, but money was tight with the commuting marriage and bureau-sized income.

Fortunately I lived near Nelson Street, the heart of black Greenville, a poor woman's Beale Street, and often would walk there after work to listen to the blues. There was nothing better than going to Doe's Eat House, where guests entered through the kitchen, ordering a coffee can full of hot tamales to go, then strolling down Nelson to catch the sound of gut-bucket loneliness slip-sliding out the juke joint doors. The Flowing

Fountain was the safest bet for good live blues, and people pretty much left you alone if you wanted to be.

If a solitary walk down Nelson Street was dangerous, I didn't know it or feel it. They say it is dangerous now. A few years after I left the Delta, crime rose dramatically. Gangs appeared on the serpentine streets of that beguiling old river town, changing its pleasantly slothful rhythm. But in 1980, I felt safe and welcome anywhere in that town. Especially on Nelson Street at night, where beer and liquor lubed a fellowship that extended to all ages and races.

Those days, when I had to walk for my music fix, were the first time I realized the similarities between hillbilly music and the blues. It was obvious, but I'd never really thought about it until then. Both dealt in heartache and lovers' angst, two things as colorblind and universal as rain. The blues might describe cheating hearts one way—*another mule's been kicking in my stall*—while country music might use different imagery—*a cold, cold heart*. But the end result, the plaintive sound, was exactly the same. The lovesick blues is the lovesick blues.

In 1983 I drove up from Jackson to the Delta for the funeral of Sam Chatmon, a celebrated blues musician. Sam was born in Bolton, Mississippi, but moved to Hollandale in 1928 and called it home the rest of his life. The son of Henderson Chatmon, an ex-slave who played fiddle for square dances and lived to be 105 years old, Sam took up guitar at age six. All of Henderson's eleven children had musical talent, as did their mother, who played piano. Chatmon's older brothers Lonnie and Bo already were known when Sam came along; the brothers famously performed with Walter Vinson as the Mississippi Sheiks.

But until the musically glorious 1960s, when folk festivals became all the rage, Sam worked on Delta plantations, accepting that music wasn't going to put beans on his plate. Though he had a long life, only part of it was spent as a musician. You might say he took music up again in retirement. So I was astounded at the number and demographic of the mourners who packed an old Hollandale school house and took turns serenading the corpse. They were mostly young white kids, younger than I, belting out the songs of Old Sam: "Brownskin Woman Blues" and "God Don't Like Ugly."

The casket was open, and from the back of the room I could see Sam's prominent nose curved just above the rim of the casket. It was surreal, the intensity of feeling that fueled the funeral music. Mourner after mourner walked forward, like Baptists to the invitational, singing tributes and tipping the proverbial hat. It was deep-down touching, the kind of spontaneous musical happening that could take place only in the Mississippi Delta, where truly the blues was born and remains in a suspended state of innocent infancy.

The best part of Sam Chatmon's funeral was that nobody seemed in charge—no preacher, no family member, no smarmy funeral home employee. It was a play without a director, and it threatened to go on into the black Delta night. I left, reluctantly, long before it was over, because I was writing on deadline. I was always writing on deadline in those days. I've often wondered who finally stepped up to Sam Chatmon's casket and said, "Enough. As great as this is, we've got to get this man into the ground." I didn't envy him the job of using the hook. Maybe the funeral wound down of its own accord. But I doubt it.

I REMEMBER THINKING THAT afternoon that Sam Chatmon's send-off wasn't that different from Hank's, when fans arrived spontaneously, paying tribute in the only reasonable way. By singing. Roy Acuff and Ernest Tubb and Red Foley and the Southwind Singers. The big names sang that day. The heavy-hitters. The *Opry* stars. Big guns from the show that had fired him. Country singers are no different from other celebrities in that respect. They recognize a photo opportunity when it bites them in the ass.

For weeks afterward, the local radio stations played Hank and more Hank, and the hoi polloi sang along. Those who hadn't made it to the funeral, and some who had made the pilgrimage but weren't seated inside. It was their turn to sing. They sang along with Hank, those mournful lyrics that suddenly took on new and deeper meaning and somehow revealed that maybe ol' Hank knew he wasn't long for this world.

Hank Williams's funeral, not unlike his music, set the gold standard. When Hank Snow died in December 1999, the Atlanta newspaper sent me to report. The funeral was long and florid, the kind country people generally expect. Open casket, musical tributes, a dozen eulogies, a video made from old home movies. And a sermon by a Missouri evangelist wearing a piano keyboard necktie.

Hank Snow's preacher son, the Reverend Jimmie Rodgers Snow, presided at a two and a half-hour memorial at the *Grand Ole Opry* house. With a name like Jimmie Rodgers Snow, you'd have to become either an evangelist or a total failure.

The crowd was mostly older. There were several wheelchairs and lots of walking canes. Country music greats like Kitty Wells and Little Jimmy Dickens sat near the front below a stage banked with flowers. Garth Brooks slipped in and sat among the fans. Marty Stuart stood for a long moment over his old friend's body, coiffed for the casket in customary toupee, dressed in a black tuxedo and gold jewelry. Snow-white roses were all around him.

Born in Nova Scotia, Hank Snow left an abusive home at age twelve to work on fishing boats. Before he became a country music star, he would toil as a painter, a cabin boy, and a Halifax street sweeper. He sold newspapers on the street and Fuller brushes door-to-door. He struggled for twenty-four years before he hit.

The long goodbye to Hank Snow was as embroidered as one of his rhinestone suits, as rich as a GooGoo Cluster. W. Bud Wendell, who was

Grand Ole Opry manager during part of Snow's fifty-year association with the show, recalled one night when a fiddler's bow rearranged Hank's toupee, and he kept singing "I'm Movin' On." Porter Wagoner did his best Hank Snow imitation, and Connie Smith sang "Peace in the Valley."

It was as grand a funeral as anyone sane would ever want. I love Hank Snow music, so don't get me wrong. But I couldn't help as I sat there over two hours to compare the two Hanks. I don't think anyone will be talking about Hank Snow's funeral in 2060. As I've said about every good country singer to come along in the last fifty-eight years, he was no Hank Williams.

CHAPTER THIRTEEN

"If you don't live it, it won't come out of your horn . . ."
— CHARLIE PARKER

Kitty Wells intended on retiring from the road and her music career at age thirty-two, in 1952, becoming a fulltime housewife, which, she told me, would have made her just as happy as being a country singer.

But the year I met her was 1995, and Kitty Wells was seventy-five and still going strong, far from retired. I caught up with her in an Atlanta suburb's civic auditorium, one of those boring, beige meeting halls that's about as far from where a honky-tonk angel would hang out as you could imagine. Back then Kitty and husband Johnny Wright were still performing three nights a week in Nashville and making as many as a hundred road trips a year.

Kitty wouldn't talk to a reporter, to me, until Johnny was by her side. And Johnny wouldn't be by her side until he sold all the CDs and T-shirts that the crowd wanted to buy. They made a non-apology apology for the delay. Garth Brooks, they said without bitterness, had made more money in a year than Kitty and Johnny made in their entire careers. So they were still out there pitching.

They stayed on the road about five more years, retiring simultaneously when Kitty was eighty. He died in 2011.

"I had really more or less retired when we came back to Nashville from Shreveport in '52," she told me. In Shreveport the Wrights used to eat fish and play cards with another *Louisiana Hayride* star, Hank Williams. But a man named J. D. Miller had written an "answer" song to Hank Thompson's popular "Wild Side of Life," the one about "honky-tonk angels." Johnny decided Kitty should record it. And record it she did. In her trademark gingham, she unwittingly became a feminist icon.

In that anthem for fairness, Kitty's plaintive voice argued: "*Too many times married men think they're still single. And they've caused many a good girl to go wrong.*"

It became a Number One country hit, the first ever for a female artist, and Kitty Wells was stuck with success, which meant staying on the road, in the game. By 1995 she'd toured all over the world—except for Australia and Japan, places Kitty said she would still like to go.

"Most people who know me know honky-tonks aren't a part of my life, but other people seem to want to hear those kinds of songs," she told me. She's a family woman first and foremost, she said. She married Wright in 1937, the same year Amelia Earhart ran out of gas. They are still together in a music world famous for D-I-V-O-R-C-E, or at least hair-pulling, plate-throwing domestic brawls like those of her late friends Hank and Audrey.

Yet nobody ever sang standards laced with the requisite hillbilly laments any better than Kitty Wells. Nobody ever sang "I Gave My Wedding Dress Away" with more pain in her voice.

Kitty told me that her friend Hank wasn't the sad sack he'd been painted as, but a fun-loving, laughing man when he was sober. Yet you can't help but contrast the lives of the two country megastars: One died early. The other soldiered on for seven decades. One lived hard. The other avoided that wild side of life and kept dust off the Bible.

ONE IMPOSSIBLE GAME MANY play, those millions of us who love Hank, is trying to figure what it might have been like if Hank had lived to a ripe old age of, say, forty, or, imagine, eighty-nine, like Roy Acuff. Or ninety-one like Kitty. Would he have kept the poignant songs coming, growing more poetic with time, or would he have eventually, like so many poets before, burned out and sold out, becoming just another has-been playing the Gulf Coast casinos or the *Opry* out of habit? Would he have embraced the so-called "new" country, which seems to some of us the antithesis of what he was about? Would he eventually have gotten around to a movie career, like Kris Kristofferson, a country music star playing a country music star? Would he have married more times than Liz Taylor, or settled in contentedly for a quiet life with Billie Jean and the *Louisiana Hayride*?

There are plenty of opinions about what might have happened if Hank had by some miracle shaken the booze he had been addicted to for half his short life, or never met the quack, Toby Marshall, who gave him pills. Marshall pretended to be a doctor who specialized in curing alcoholics; he was really a veteran of two prison terms, one for armed robbery, who used chloral hydrate and a bogus prescription pad for his "cure."

The big "IF" doesn't stop the conjecture.

The late Chet Atkins told the Griersons he believed Hank peaked before he died. "He was right at the zenith of his writing and creative career," Atkins said. "He was on the downward slope, but he would have written some great songs now and then anyway. Of course, all of this is just hypothetical. Who knows?"

A Jackson, Mississippi, attorney and amateur musician whom I believe I'll leave nameless cheerfully described to Pat Grierson a game he and his band members played. "We've got this game: *The Hank Williams Burnout*, we call it. Each player has to remember one verse of a Hank Williams song. Whoever can't remember first has to buy drinks for everybody . . ."

Hugh Harris, the Hank impersonator, spends more time than most wondering what would have happened had Hank lived longer. He inhabits the role, but hopes for a different ending. "I think it would have had some effect on the music industry, but exactly in which direction?" Hugh muses.

"Would he have grown 'wilder,' musically speaking, and been one of the early rock performers instead of a rock influence? Or, would rock and roll have grown more slowly, with Hank reining it closer to traditional country. No one can say for sure, but the course of music could not have been the same . . ."

I, for once, have no opinion. I used to think about but never wrote a novel with its hero a country music star who shot to fame on merit, lost his emotional footing, and became a recluse who played music only to the trees and critters around the cave where he chose to live. I decided the story line lacked verisimilitude. Nobody who strove for success like Hank would simply retreat. To a cave. Bad idea. He would keep entertaining, or die trying.

And that, of course, was what happened. There is really no "if he had lived" to the story. The only real question was "How long could he last?" The inimitable talent was his master, as much or more than the whiskey, and it drove him like a teenager drives his daddy's car. Flat out. True talent is not unlike a prison sentence. You can do good time or hard time, but do it you must.

Every credible Hank biography I've read has indicated the man knew how talented he was. He could be downright cocky, in fact. And he could judge his own work, not something of which every artist is capable. He knew, for instance, that "On the Banks of the Old Pontchartrain," was weak. Hank famously sang it, of course, but bought the song from its author, Kathleen Ramona Vincent. He often held "Pontchartrain" up as an example of what *not* to do.

So it would have bothered him no end if, in time, his writing skills suffered because of the alcoholism, the drugs, the personal angst that buffeted Hank all his life. He would have been his own worst critic, a character not unlike one Jeff Bridges played so convincingly in the movie "Crazy Heart." Maybe it was best he went out with hits in the can.

A better question than the one about his living a longer life is this: Why does the *music* live so long after his death, fresh as the day it was first written and sung? How could one man master a genre and hold the record forever? How did Hank do what he did, and why has his reputation grown surely and steadily for nearly six decades?

Willie Nelson told me in a 2002 phone interview that nobody, but nobody, should ever expect to surpass Hank Williams. "Nobody should even *want* to. Anything we do that Hank already did will be less, so we have to try to do something else."

And Willie has certainly done *something else* better than *anyone else*.

THERE WAS AN ELEMENT of luck in the fact Hank made music at all. We think of genius as inexorable, water running downhill. But I suppose it really is not. In 1942 Hank Williams, age nineteen, went to work at a Mobile shipyard. The wartime army didn't want him. He had to make a living. Jimmy Buffett's mother, Peets Buffett, unearthed Hank's application years ago while sorting old files at Alabama Dry Dock & Shipbuilding Company. I got to see a copy.

There was something almost startling about seeing Hank's actual handwriting, akin to looking at Charlotte Bronte's longhand manuscript of *Jane Eyre* in the British Museum. Hank wrote in a sloppy hand on the official job application.

"Williams, Hiram Hank," he wrote. For his address he scrawled, "none yet." Hank said he weighed 136 pounds, "without overcoat or hat," as the paper specified. He must have been fudging a little, judging from early photos where he looks as thin as Kate Moss.

Color of hair? "Brown." Color of eyes? "Brown." Complexion? "Sallow."

Young Hank must have been a little nervous when handed the thorough, four-page document that asked the name and address of "all members of your immediate family, including immediate relatives of your wife." The application had been designed in wartime with an eagle eye for enemy sympathizers who might divulge secrets of the dock.

"Have you ever worked in a foreign country?" That was Question 25. "Yes," Hank answered. In Mexico in 1940 as a musician. Hank's honest nature was apparent, even in this bureaucratic format. He marked "No" when asked if he'd ever had a physical exam. And to Question 23, "Have you ever been arrested?," he wrote "Yes. Suspicion (sic), last year, Montgomery, mistake."

So here was a kid who had been around—or to jail and Mexico, at least. Now he was cooling his heels in a strange town, staying with his uncle Bob, playing nights in waterfront taverns and, some say, sleeping on the day job. Hank listed music as his hobby and said he had attended high school in Montgomery but never graduated, that he'd taken a bookkeeping course at a business college, and been employed as a weekend painter and a musician at WSFA and WCOV radio stations in Montgomery.

Why did he leave those jobs? "Contract ran out," Hank answered. And he would leave the shipyard job in short order, as well, after only three months working for sixty-six cents an hour as a ship-fitter's helper. Hank told his bosses he needed to be closer to his mother, who was ill, and to his sister. The company wanted medical proof. Judging from pictures of the robust matron at the time, I would have required proof, too.

Thank goodness Hank didn't waste much time welding widgets. His bossy mother did him and the rest of the world a huge favor when she came to fetch Hank home. The story is not unlike that of the job the great cartoonist Charles Schulz almost accepted after the war: lettering tombstones.

Hank also managed in his twenty-nine years to influence a whole generation of country singers. George Jones, when first starting to perform, rode around with a cardboard cutout of Hank in his car. Roy Clark once saw Hank perform in Baltimore and sat, chin on the stage, awestruck over what he was witnessing. At some point in the show, Hank broke a guitar string. Instead of handing off his guitar and letting someone else do the menial labor, Hank turned it over to his Drifting Cowboys and went off to one corner of the stage to change the string himself. When he looked up, he saw the entire audience had followed him with their eyes. "Haven't you ever seen someone change a guitar string before?" he joked.

Roy Clark never forgot that moment.

Porter Wagoner once pointed out to Jett Williams the exact Ryman pew where he sat as a boy and first heard Hank sing "Lovesick Blues," not coincidentally the same day Porter decided to become a country singer himself. "You'll never make it," Porter's own mother told her son. That story makes Lillian Williams look good by comparison.

Pulitzer Prize-winning author David Halberstam played the "What if?" game in a *Look* magazine essay in July, 1971. Kris Kristofferson is on that magazine cover, and the headline story is this: "Hillbilly No More: Country Music Sweeps the U.S.A." The large-format *Look*, incidentally, cost thirty-five cents.

"Can it be that he would be forty-seven this year?" Halberstam wrote. "And what would he be like now—bald, pudgy in the middle, his sharp, reedy voice gone mellow, his songs backed by violins, pianos, and worse? On late-night talk shows beamed from New York and dressed in Continental-cut suits? No, it is inconceivable . . ."

Halberstam concludes that Hank was a comet, with "the legend of the comet lasting longer in our folk history than if somehow they had managed to discipline that raw talent, temper his passions, assuage his fears and turn him into just another middle-aged singer."

SHARON THOMASON, A GEORGIA writer and friend, reminded me of that issue of *Look*, which she has, and Don had. Don kept his in a special place on our bookshelves. Sharon has just completed a book called *Sing Them*

Over Again to Me: A Memoir of Enjoying Classic Country Music and has an encyclopedic knowledge of the genre. It's her passion. And she'd be about like any other die-hard classic country music fan except for her incredible store of trivia and contacts.

"Now we have to think what Hank would be like at eighty-seven," she says, extending Halberstam's point. But somehow, at least to me, the thought of Hank as an old man isn't as disturbing to me as Hank at middle age. He was born old.

I polled Sharon as well, asking her if our hero Hank would have had a problem with drums "all up in your face," as the bluegrass master Larry Cordle sang about in "Murder on Music Row." *Someone killed country music, cut out its heart and soul.*

Or how would Hank have reacted to hyped, *Hee Haw*-type television, or over-produced and endless award shows? What would he have made of the smoother sounds (think Glen Campbell) that took over once he was gone from the scene?

"Hank and his music were so timeless, I can't imagine that he would have had a problem with drums," Sharon says as a for-instance. "I believe Ernest Tubb was first to use them on the *Opry*, and they really didn't change his music that much. Or *Hee Haw*. Hank's radio banter sounds a little like some of the *Hee Haw* stuff, doesn't it? Glen Campbell—that's another story. The genius of Hank Williams's music is that it was so country and yet so universal . . ."

If—and again, that's a big one—Hank had lived, I like to think he would have aged gracefully, a la Willie Nelson, graciously singing duets with the good young talents as they happened by—Kristofferson, Willie, Lucinda Williams, Iris DeMent. And maybe with some of his old friends, the ones who cried real tears when he died, Kitty Wells and Ray Price.

"Hank was top dog then, and he still is," Ray Price told me one January night in 2001. It was his birthday; he had a cold. Once a Nashville roommate with Hank, Price turned seventy-five on the road and under the weather.

"They haven't been able to hide that part of country music," he said. Price, like Kitty Wells, tempered his lifestyle and has lived to grow philosophical about it. His first Number One hit came three years after his friend Hank died, in 1956, when "Crazy Arms" stayed on the charts for forty-five weeks. In 1970, his cover of Kristofferson's "For the Good Times" sold eleven million copies.

Price worked hard to forge his own distinctive sound, even though the remnants of Hank's Drifting Cowboys formed his new band. He called his band the Cherokee Cowboys. Price added strings and polish to songs with traditional country themes. It wasn't a move that thrilled hillbilly purists. Critics said he was Perry Como with a cowlick, that he took gut-felt songs and put them through a Waring blender. But his "maverick" approach has stood him in good stead over five decades. It might not have been what Hank would have done, but Willie has already told us there's no sense in trying that.

"I never laid eyes on the man, but he influenced me more than any other writer/performer in history," Whispering Bill Anderson says of Hank, without qualification.

In his 1989 autobiography, Anderson related an incident at the University of Georgia during the mid-1950s. He was there to study journalism, thinking sports reporting might be a good fallback job after his baseball career wound down. And, he wrote, he chose journalism because to major in journalism you didn't have to take a math course.

> In fact, in my sixteen years of schooling I flunked only two subjects: math and music! (Actually, the music course I failed was called Music Appreciation. One day the professor was telling the class something about Beethoven and I asked how that compared

to something Hank Williams had once done, and he roared that I was never even so much as to mention the name Hank Williams in the same breath with Beethoven again. I decided not to return to Music Appreciation class after that. It was obvious I didn't appreciate their music and they darn sure didn't appreciate mine!) Of course, math and music are the only two things from school that I've used since I got out!

In a book by Harold C. Schonberg called *The Lives of the Great Composers,* the author describes Beethoven this way: "He was of a special breed and he knew it. He also knew he was writing for eternity . . ."

I'd say that description fits Hank as well as Ludwig. Anderson's "Appreciate this!" to that high-and-mighty professor seems anachronistic now, considering Hank's won a Pulitzer Prize and stood a test harder than any dunderhead might have been given at the University of Georgia: the test of time.

CHAPTER FOURTEEN

*"Love is the greatest gift, but music is surely a close
second. Combine the two and you move to the highest
level of human experience . . ."*

— Robert Khayat, amateur musician and
Chancellor Emeritus, University of Mississippi

The headline read: "When nobody screams 'I wanna hold your hand.'" The date was March 1987, and the column beneath that clever head was supposed to be funny. It was inspired by a visit to Memphis by Ringo Starr, who had been spotted at a popular watering hole called the Bombay Bicycle Club, dining alone.

And I was off.

It's strange that the most negative attention I ever got for a single column in three decades of writing columns—and that includes a lot of essays about politics, abortion, gun control, and never on the side of the Southern conservative majority—was one about music.

It was a slow news day, and I sat on my friend Laura Coleman's bedroom floor in Memphis, probably not feeling great because whenever I made it to the big city I tended to stay up too late enjoying newspaper colleagues I didn't get to see often. I lived at the time in Counce, Tennessee, a papermill town near Pickwick Lake. In those days I wrote four columns a week, so one was almost always due. When I saw the story about Ringo, I recognized the germ of an idea.

And I wrote about the irony of Ringo, sitting alone and unmolested, when two decades earlier the Beatles had stood the city on its ear. *"Ringo no longer has girls following him everywhere he goes, screaming and trying to pluck his eyebrows for souvenirs . . ."*

I said that as a kid he'd been my favorite Beatle because in any situation I always choose the underdog, the runt of the litter. I called him the most untalented of the Fab Four, which I assumed was conventional wisdom, and the least good-looking. I concluded—and this is what the Memphis television news anchors quoted again and again—"An aging Beatle is yesterday's news."

I didn't mention that it was in Memphis in 1966 when the "more popular than Jesus" controversy came to a head. John Lennon had told a British journalist that the Beatles had done just that, grown bigger and more influential than Jesus, that is to say religion, which didn't cause a ripple of a reaction in England. But when an American teen magazine reprinted the quote, all hell broke loose.

The Memphis City Council voted to cancel a Beatles concert scheduled at Mid-South Coliseum later that year. "The Beatles are not welcome in Memphis," they decreed. A local minister planned a Christian rally, which, he said, "would give the youth of the Mid-South an opportunity to show Jesus Christ is more popular than The Beatles." When the show did take place—money trumped the council—a firecracker set off on stage caused a minor panic. The singers understandably thought they were targets of gunfire.

But I didn't get into all the Beatle-burning stuff from the past. I just mused that the white-hot attention that once nipped at the Fab Four's heels was no longer a major nuisance, at least not for Ringo. A simple, some might say simplistic, thesis.

Ringo had business in Memphis. He had come to town to record with celebrated producer and songwriter Chips Moman. In their efforts to reboot the Memphis music industry, the city fathers had given Moman the keys of the city and one-dollar-a-year recording space in an old fire station. In usual Memphis fashion, politicians were wetting all over themselves like so many over-eager puppies. They were convinced that Moman, who had left Memphis in a huff once already in the 1970s, was the new city savior, come to resurrect Memphis from its economic doldrums. His advance billing proved impossible to live up to, and the failure that inevitably followed was not altogether Moman's fault.

I believe now that by 1987 Chips was looking for somebody, anybody, to scapegoat his impending free-fall. By 1990, he would have filed for bankruptcy after being sued by the First Tennessee National Association for allegedly defaulting on $2 million in loans. He spent seven days in jail for refusing a court order to return disputed recording equipment to the studio. And, most interesting to me, Ringo Starr was fighting the release of the Memphis recording, which the former Beatle said was sub-par.

The Monday the column appeared, however, Moman still had plenty of sway. His problems had not yet become public. He telephoned me. I was home in Counce by the time the column appeared, a good thing. It gave me a hundred miles of buffer.

"You are a piece of shit," he said. "And I hope your husband hears." He said I was through in Memphis journalism, wait and see. Then he called a press conference, threatening to whip one of the *Commercial Appeal* reporters who showed up to cover it. The next day he led a protest march outside the newspaper office. About sixty people, including several prominent Memphis musicians, showed up with signs: *"Malice Towards Music." "Ringo Beat Goes On." "Rheta, We Want You in an Octopus' Garden."* About twenty people canceled their subscriptions.

Local television news, delighted with the tempest, led with the story that evening. Local radio stations, where Moman had friends, played a customized Beatles song: *Ugly Rheta the Meter Maid.* David Brown, my editor, stood behind me and the column, to his credit, but fanned the flames when he thanked me publicly and tongue-in-cheek for reminding everyone who Ringo was.

The contrived controversy died, as all do, and was all but forgotten by the time Chips was sued by Ringo, who won a court injunction to stop the release of the album produced at the ill-fated Three Alarm Studio. Starr claimed he, Chips, and the studio musicians and everyone else involved had been drunk or high for most of the recording sessions. Moman left Memphis once again.

BLAMING ME FOR SABOTAGING the Memphis music industry was a little like blaming a housefly for adding the extra weight that sunk the Titanic. I've learned you can never anticipate reaction to a column—it's always the "harmless" throwaways that provoke the anger that blindsides you—but to be considered the enemy of music anywhere hurt my feelings more than a little. I'd always championed music in the column, especially of the Southern persuasion. Traditional country love was my chief passion, but I also was drawn to the blues. So many of the artists were still *living* the blues.

While reporting from the Memphis newspaper's bureau in Greenville, Mississippi, I befriended a blues singer named Son House. Son lived in nearby Leland in a two-room hovel on Sinclair Street. Photographs of Son performing all over papered the walls. Son singing the blues in England, in the White House, in the Delta. Some were framed, some not. Some hung straight, some not. In the small front room was a sagging bed, its blue coverlet so old the chenille bubbles had burst. There was a black-and-white television that always seemed to be playing *Benson* reruns.

The most fascinating thing about the house—other than its famous occupant—were clay sculptures that Son fashioned from the Yazoo gumbo. He gave me one as gift. A corpse in a brick coffin. Son Thomas eventually would be "adopted" by blues enthusiasts and academics from

Ole Miss, but at the time I knew him he was just scraping by. Once when he was playing for a big Republican soiree down in Jackson, the power company came by to cut off his power. He'd been singing all his life, with nothing to show for it but a bottomless well of material. Hard times. Faithless women. Broken dreams. He'd been shot at by angry husbands and hounded by bill collectors. He knew his subject.

One of my favorite music columns got written almost by accident. I had been to the annual fair at the Choctaw reservation near Philadelphia, Mississippi, when someone told me about a songwriter named Bob Ferguson who lived there. You may not know his name, but you've heard his song. Ferlin Husky recorded it first, leaving out the verse that called Jesus by name so the song could play on honky-tonk jukeboxes. George Beverly Shea sang it, Jesus and all, at countless Billy Graham crusades. Kitty White gave it the rhythm and blues treatment. And perhaps best of all, the actor Robert Duvall sang it while tapping one boot in the sweet, low-budget movie *Tender Mercies*.

Bob Ferguson scribbled the lyrics to "The Wings of a Dove" on a brown paper bag as he drove between work and his Nashville home one day in 1958. He was a Tennessee state employee then, filming fifteen-minute television shows called "The World Outdoors" for the Game and Fish Commission. That evening he felt elated because he'd met a film deadline. "I had this burst of elation, this prayer," he told me in 1985. The result was a song, a simple classic that sold more than ten million copies and stayed on the top of both pop and country charts in 1959 for thirty-six weeks. It was translated into Swedish and German and distributed worldwide. It was heralded by the Catholic church, but banned in England—why, Ferguson still didn't know.

His old friend Ferlin Husky happened to invite him over for Easter dinner in 1958. "We sat around singing and talking, and I sang him the song I had written," he recalled. Before they wound down, Ferlin asked,

"Sing that bird song again." Ferguson did.

"Bob, that's a hit," the singer said. "Not a country hit. A Top 10, pop, country, smash hit."

Ferguson said Husky asked if he could record it, "and I didn't say 'no.'"

After Ferguson fell in love with a Choctaw woman named Martha, he moved to Mississippi and made films for the Indians. He said people everywhere had relayed stories about how "Wings" comforted them in bad times. He was not particularly religious—"I have spurts"—but he was pleased the "bird song" meant something to somebody."

One day I was lucky enough to find myself judging the Fayette County Egg Festival's World Chicken Beauty Contest in Somerville, Tennessee, along with the local funeral home director, a grocer, the sheriff, and Mr. Funky Chicken himself, Memphis bluesman Rufus Thomas. There were more of us judges than there were chickens.

You know you've arrived as a serious journalist when you are judging the best of four chickens. They didn't really need the CPA who tallied the scores. Little Miss Egg Festival could have figured it out on her fingers.

A chicken named Granny Clampett won the gleaming, four-foot-high trophy. I couldn't vote for her because of the erroneous moniker. Granny, of *The Beverly Hillbillies* fame, was a Moses. Daisy Moses. She was Jed Clampett's mother-in-law, not his mother. Details, details.

The contest was late starting so we mostly sat around and listened to Rufus Thomas talk about being famous. You can't go anywhere anonymously, he complained in a good-natured way. "I went to this place out in the country a long, long time ago. You went through a gate, and they locked it behind you. There was whiskey-drinking and gambling inside . . . And I walked into the room and folks over there in a corner right away started hollering, 'Hey, there, Rufus.' I ducked out of there fast."

Fans kept coming by asking Rufus to sing. One beauty operator offered to cut his hair. "You'd have to find it first," he said, and laughed a big laugh. A woman from a nearby refreshment booth offered him a couple of homemade brownies. He carefully put them with a bunch of foil-wrapped rib bones he planned to take home for his dog.

Finally, we did our judging. Miss Egg Festival crowned the World Chicken Beauty. As a surprise, they presented Rufus Thomas with one of the contestants, a big, white rooster dressed as Jesse James. "Be cool, chicken, now be cool," Rufus told the rooster, which probably didn't understand why it was being held up to a throbbing microphone as a strange man boomed his thanks.

As I was leaving, I looked back. The gregarious old singer was standing in the middle of his admirers, holding a white rooster under one arm. The rooster was wearing six-shooters and a cowboy hat and, no longer cool, was flapping about wildly.

Fame is a strange bird.

CHAPTER FIFTEEN

*"Every tattoo shop has Hank Sr., Hank Jr., and Hank III
playing in the shop."*
— CHARLES TAYLOR, TATTOO ARTIST AND ORGANIZER
OF THE LOST HIGHWAY TATTOO MUSIC EXPO

Politics and Hank Williams make strange bedfellows.
I guess that's always the way when a musician or any person
reaches legend status. The rank and file, the ones who "brung"
him, must turn over the hero to "experts." An impressionist masterpiece
becomes a paint-by-number, every shadow and nuance assigned a color
applied within the lines.

It has happened to Hank. And to Elvis. In August 1995, the week after
the University of Mississippi held its annual William Faulkner conference—It has happened to Faulkner, too, of course—Elvis was given the
academic treatment: the "International Conference on Elvis Presley. In
Search of Elvis: Music, Race, Religion, Art, Performance." If the title of the
conference had gotten much longer, they could have wrapped it around
Oxford's storied courthouse square.

I remember my initial reaction: Say what?

I went, of course. The Atlanta newspaper correctly thought it would
make good column fodder falling under the category "so bad it's good." I
was, to say the least, somewhat dubious about Ole Miss giving the asparagus finger sandwich treatment to poor dead Elvis, who had done okay so
far hanging out in trailer parks. "Asparagus finger sandwich" was what
Don muttered when told of any fancy-pants gathering. He had at some

point attended a swell luncheon, in Oxford, as it happens, that had on its menu asparagus finger sandwiches. Hush my mouth and pass the Duke's.

Someone wise once said that everything in the social sciences is either obvious or untrue. That quote leapt to mind, though the Elvis conference was brought to us by the English department, which ought to have known better.

It took a righteous sermon to change my mind about a conference based on dead Elvis. The Reverend Will Campbell could convert anyone to any position. Campbell is a Mississippi native, a Tennessee author, and a rare bird—a Southern white preacher who acted like a Christian during the civil rights era. His lecture, or sermon—he thundered—that day was called "Rednecks," and was a brilliant defense of poor working whites like the Presleys of Tupelo, or the Williamses of Montgomery.

"Being from poor, rural stock did not make Mr. Presley a bigot. Race has been the trump card used to keep poor blacks and poor whites enemies," Preacher Campbell roared. "Where did poor working whites get the idea that being white meant being superior?"

They got the idea, he said, from the "fulminations" of self-serving political leaders like the late Mississippi Governor Ross Barnett, who effectively incited a riot and "turned this very campus into a war zone." He didn't stop with ancient history. Remember, the year was 1995. The same thing was going on, Campbell said, with "poor whites buying into the fraud called the 'Contract With America.'" The United States in his opinion was moving toward a fascist theocracy, and if you didn't believe it turn on the TV and watch the "right-wing, electronic soul-molesters who preach 'Take up your cross and get rich.' I don't know where this country is headed, but I know there comes a time to fret and be worried."

Amen, I thought. Amen.

Hank, not unlike Elvis, has had his share of academic interpreters, most of whom weren't as wise and canny and funny as Campbell. I now have read four times a scholarly essay in a 1985 issue of *The South At-lantic Quarterly* that uses as its title the name of a Hank song that I love. I'm missing something. I can't make heads or tails of the author's the-sis—something about the disillusionment of Americans as evidenced by popular culture—but I love the fact some professor used "Pictures from Life's Other Side" to draw an audience. Must have seemed like an exotic hook to use in academic circles, especially when the other essays in the *Quarterly* had titles like: "The Problem of Moral Judgments in History" and "Restoring the American Dream; The Agrarian-Decentralist Move-ment, 1930–1946." Pictures from life's other side. Brilliant.

Hank has risen to such heights that people argue every aspect of his life and its meaning. Not unlike the way folks argue about their bibles and religion, Hank purists disagree about all kinds of minutia. My friend Jerry Elijah Brown has a wonderful observation about religious arguments in his book called *Alabama's Mitcham Wars*:

> Should the hymns of Isaac Watts be allowed? Was Moses actually found in the bulrushes? Is it a sin to cook on Sunday? Once-saved-always-saved, or is back-sliding allowed? If people wanted to find a forum to elevate animosities to some higher plane, they found it (and still find it) in religion . . .

Same thing with Hank. The debates rage. What role did Audrey play in Hank's success? Was she the ambition behind Hank's talent, or simply the inspiration for the cheating songs? Was it Tee-Tot the black street singer or, *au contraire*, shaped-note, "sacred harp," singing schools in Baptist churches that first influenced Hank? In other words, God or mammon? Was mother Lillian mean and domineering or simply protective and supportive? Would Hank have returned to Audrey and the *Opry* had he lived longer? Or would he have dug in and fattened up with Billie Jean and her Louisiana kin to live a long and contented life?

We won't even get to the endless debates about his death, which range from "Was it New Year's Eve or New Year's Day?" to elaborate murder conspiracies.

One vivid example of the Hank hair-splitting only destined to grow worse with the decades is the search for the *real* Rufus Payne, the street musician everyone called Tee-Tot. "Almost everything that I've read about Rufus Payne has included inaccurate or erroneous information, and has been published in newspapers, historical and genealogical periodicals, and on the Internet for all the world to see," Judy Atkins Taylor wrote in the *Butler County Historical and Genealogical Society Quarterly*. Her research thoroughly refuted that of Alice K. Harp who wrote for Montgomery's genealogical quarterly and contended Rufus Payne grew up in New Orleans, first learned jazz piano, and was a sophisticated showman who used the front door to play big parties at big houses while Hank tagged along and came in through the kitchen. How's that for convenient irony? Ms. Harps admits she has no idea why, as "the equivalent of today's rock/rap stars" in the Big City, such a supposed jazz professor as Tee-Tot would migrate to less cosmopolitan Butler County, Alabama, where he mostly played on the streets.

I'm afraid one of the historians has the wrong Rufus Payne, and it would appear to be the one with the more fanciful story. Tee-Tot was surely Butler County born and bred and not some superstar New Orleans transplant slumming in Greenville, Alabama. That's my educated guess.

But there I go, delving into the minutia that I find largely unimportant, at least for my purposes. It is easy to be seduced by the silliness of shaping artists we love into huggable stereotypes. Maybe it's not so much paint-by-number we want as black and white, good and evil, right and wrong, hero and villain.

I realized something about myself when I got heavily into writing this book—if you don't realize something about yourself while writing a book you probably haven't invested much thought. My personal epiphany was this: I have an embarrassing lack of interest in the genealogical tributaries that feed my own life, much less Hank's. To start this book I reread all the biographies, good and bad, and Googled myself silly. Folks sent me articles, scholarly and un-, feeding me more information than I'd ever known was available about Hank.

I found it far more helpful to listen, again and again, to the music. And if, at this reading, you are saying, "Oh, sure, that's a fine excuse to sit about on your lazy rear end all day and listen to Hank," then you are a perceptive soul. That certainly was part of it, part of the enjoyment of devoting a year to Hank. But I can make the case that his music stands alone, like the nursery rhyme cheese, gleeful or sad, supporting not only Hank's short life but millions of other lives, folk like my father and myself who could not get over the relevance of the lyrics and sounds to our own common existences. We needed Hank the way some need bottled oxygen to supplement their lungs.

As interesting as Hank's short life was, I'm not all that concerned with the torturous details of his marriages or death, or, for that matter, his life, at least not his life outside the music. I feel somewhat like the Georgia short story writer Mary Hood, whose character didn't want to ruin the heavens for herself by learning the names of all the constellations. She wanted, as country singer Iris DeMent sang in a similar vein, "to let the mystery be."

'Tis human to speculate, of course. If I wanted to make any leap of interpretation about ol' Hank that would suit myself, one based on hopes and not facts, I'd imagine his politics if he'd lived till 2011. And they would be liberal. Nobody who wrote like Hank and grew up dirt poor could contort into a right wing posture. I believe that. A 2011 Hank would be liberal, or at least what passes for liberal in today's parlance. By liberal I mean this: he would care about others. Unlike his son, who campaigned for Sarah Palin in 2008 and routinely embarrasses himself and his father's name, unlike a myriad of country stars to the contrary, I like to think Hank would remember and relish his roots.

I think about one of my other all-time heroes, reporter Ernie Pyle, who didn't make it back from World War II for the Eisenhower years or any of the subsequent political eras that would follow. In 1995 I asked his buddy, the late cartoonist Bill Mauldin, what side of the philosophical fence he figured Ernie might have landed on had he lived to old age, or at least lived to return home from war. Mauldin said what I wanted to hear. Ernie would have been so liberal as a peacetime columnist he would have been shunned by those who adored his grunt-friendly wartime correspondence, Mauldin said. How did he figure? Easy. It had happened to him.

Mauldin returned from World War II a winner at age twenty-three of his first Pulitzer Prize, the meaning of which he had had to have explained to him when he won it. He thought championing of the Little Guy would go over well at home the same way it had from overseas. It did not. The trenchant commentary of Willie and Joe was too downbeat for a peacetime America that wanted to hear only the best about itself under Eisenhower stars. The cartoonist had planned for Willie and Joe to be killed the day the war ended. But his syndicate persuaded him to save their potentially lucrative lives. Then syndicate editors proceeded to "soften" his views.

"It was selling like hot cakes, because I had become famous. But then I lost newspapers as fast as I gained them," he said with a wry laugh. He soon let go of Willie and Joe and embraced his fate as an editorial cartoonist—a liberal one who won a second Pulitzer.

I like to think Hank would have been saving family farms with Willie Nelson, not looking askance at Russia from Sarah Palin's back yard. But that's just me. And that kind of conjecture is irritating even when I'm the one with the dream. Bottom line: nobody knows.

Hank never had to choose sides in the incendiary times of racial unrest in Alabama and the South. Just as he never had to hear rock and roll called country and country called passé and fiddles replaced with drums. He won his purity of potential the hard way. Hank died.

CHAPTER SIXTEEN

When griping grief the heart doth wound,
and doleful dumps the mind oppresses,
then music, with her silver sound,
with speedy help doth lend redress.

— WILLIAM SHAKESPEARE

W hen dogs are young, they have the whitest teeth. Nothing's prettier than puppy teeth. As they age, of course, the dog's teeth yellow and crumble, often to the nub, and, until recently, nobody did a thing about it. One dog with whom I had a long acquaintance used to chew on rocks. Dogs, not unlike their human masters, can be their own worst enemies.

Today's veterinarians don't miss a trick or a nickel. Nowadays they nag you to put your dog to sleep once a year for a thorough tooth-cleaning. I always hesitate, reasoning that maybe anesthesia is harder on a dog, especially an old one, than tooth decay.

Like every other canine body part, dog teeth age the same as humans, only a lot faster. Seven times faster, some say. Thus anyone who has owned a dog has seen time-lapse of his own mortality.

There's this one photo of Hank included in the liner notes of *The Unreleased Recordings*. It's the happiest-looking photo of Hank I've ever seen. He's wearing a white hat, a white shirt and coat, and a wide necktie adorned with a pen-and-ink cowboy doing some fancy roping. He's holding a bag of Mother's Best flour on his shoulder. His eyes look clear, his handsome face is unlined and his teeth are straight, white, and young.

Considering his spotty diet—I heard one man who swore he saw Hank Williams at a country store in Pine Level, Alabama, eating an onion with a piece of pound cake—they are beautiful teeth. They look like what they were: a very young man's teeth.

For some reason, that happy Hank photo with the sparkling teeth makes me incredibly sad. A man with teeth like that was too young to die. So much is made of how much older than his years Hank looked and sounded, and all that's true. But, by god, the teeth don't lie. He had pretty puppy teeth. He should have had a few more years.

I could stare at that photograph for hours, feeling alternately glad and sad. Glad that Hank's life wasn't all gloom and doom. Sad that he didn't live longer to enjoy more of it.

After Don died in 2009, I worried I would no longer be able to enjoy music. That happens sometimes to people when they grieve. I have it on good authority. They give up music, bury it with the dead. The genius cartoonist Charles Schulz told me he couldn't even *listen* to music when he was depressed, and depression was a regular part of his life. Some of his children deny that now, but I know what he told me. I spent a good bit of time with Schulz in 1988 working on an authorized biography for the book division of the syndicate that published "Peanuts." He had veto power over every word I wrote, and he endorsed what I wrote about his depression. Twice, because we republished in paperback several years later. But that's another story.

Suffice to say, Schulz was a good and decent man. I loved him. Our musical tastes were worlds apart, however. He listened to classical instead of the roots music I favor. He liked a smooth, orchestrated sound. He thought, for instance, that Joni James's rendition of "Cold, Cold Heart" was the ultimate. Her un-country album of Hank songs, in fact, was the way Schulz "discovered" Hank. To my ear, the Joni James version is so anemic and polished that one has to wonder why Schulz thought Hank mattered. Joni couldn't even bring herself to drop the "g" from "Your Cheatin' Heart" when she sang that song.

I suspect that Schulz appreciated most its words. Words were his business, after all. He often worked a strip around a word or proper name that he found interesting. And the artist was so sensitive to sound that he mapped out entire animated television specials to use certain hymns that he loved. I sent him a cassette tape of the musical trio Dolly Parton, Linda Ronstadt, and Emmylou Harris singing the old hymn "Farther Along." He liked it and worked it into an animated special about cancer.

Music mattered a lot to him when he felt upbeat enough to enjoy it. And his love of good music showed itself in the great writing that characterized the fifty years of his celebrated comic strip. Good writing has rhythm. Everyone serious about the writing business knows that.

It mattered so much that his keen mind and rather timorous personality couldn't handle the beauty of music when he was feeling melancholy. I understood what he was saying, or so I thought. But at that point in my life, I'd never been so sad that music didn't help. But when Don died, I worried about that right away. Would it be the day my music died?

I decided without much internal debate that only Hank music would be played at Don's outdoor memorial. Hank Williams had been the love of his musical life. But, I'll admit, I hesitated briefly. What if forever after Hank's songs served only to remind me of that fresh, stinging ache that was part of the aftermath of Don's death? What if "Mind Your Own Business," for an instance, no longer brought back fond memories of Eduardo and Heloisa's funny, summer wedding with its arbor of blue hydrangea and rented china? What if "Cold, Cold Heart" no longer reminded me of a first date but a last rite? What if instead of finding comfort in those familiar songs that had been part of my life my whole life I suddenly felt low and melancholy whenever Hank sang them? What if Hank songs became the soundtrack for my private hell?

It didn't work that way. And I remain grateful. Instead of adding to the ache, Hank absorbed part of the blow for me. It was as if he articulated the grief that for me was unspeakable. He not only spoke of it, he made it somehow beautiful. Grief and loss are part of life for those of us who live more than a few years. And to help with it, to change and beautify it, like Rapunzel spinning straw into gold, that was Hank's rare gift.

I was like my father in that respect. I needed music. Never more than when I hurt. For better, for worse. Especially for worse. Unlike Schulz, I not only handled it, I craved it. And not just Hank, though he worked the hardest at easing my pain, and, as usual, did the best job. I started listening to singers I'd barely even heard of before. Lucinda Williams, no relation to Hank but daughter of the poet Miller Williams, was my new favorite. She had a song called "Lake Charles" on her celebrated—and by now old—*Car Wheels on a Grave Road* album. I'd heard of the album but never heard the album. There is a difference. By changing a few of the proper nouns—Lake Charles to Henderson (Louisiana), Nacogdoches to Moss Point—I could make the song about Don. *He used to talk about it. He always said Louisiana was where he felt at home.* I must have listened to that song ten thousand times. I didn't visit a grave as some new widows do—there was no grave to visit—I played Lucinda, whose voice, like Hank's, held hurt.

Music was medicinal now.

AFTER DON'S DEATH IN late March, I tried to decide what to do with the ashes that came from the funeral home in an ugly plastic container that I kept in the dark bottom of a living room cabinet. I saw a cornball movie in which a widow, played by Jessica Lange, makes a cross-country odyssey to deliver her husband's ashes to his daughter, who is insistent on burying them. Along the way, the widow scattered the ashes in several different places that had been important to the couple, arriving at the step-daughter's memorial service with no ashes left. It was a weak movie but a good idea, I thought. It hurt less somehow to scatter democratically amongst the different places Don had loved. It was a less definitive, therefore less traumatic, commitment.

In grief you grasp at straws.

In September I drove from north Mississippi to south Louisiana, alone except for my yellow dog Mabel, to scatter most of Don's ashes in the Atchafalaya Basin. That felt right. Not much did. Later I would take a few with me to France and throw them in the Seine. Don loved France. I also put some around Don's kumquat tree in our Henderson, Louisiana, yard before selling the house. He always checked for fruit on that tree first thing when we'd arrive. I dropped some ashes in the branch by the house in Mississippi near a bridge he built me for an anniversary present. And a few I kept, keep, in a small piece of Shearwater pottery on the bookshelf. Shearwater pottery from the Mississippi Gulf Coast was our favorite, the color of the ocean at sunset, and made at the Anderson compound in Don's home county of Jackson.

I don't keep up with such dates, but, in a wonderful coincidence, the day I made it to the swamp was the first day of duck season. Don would have appreciated the timing. He planned his life around getting to the swamp by duck season; the least I could do was get him there in death.

I drove all day, alternately singing along with Lucinda or Hank, and crying, stopping every hour or so to walk Mabel or to get something to drink. Frequent stops made a long trip longer. It was almost sunset before I pulled into Henderson. I didn't stop in town to visit the usual suspects, our good friends Jeanette and Johnell Latiolais. Instead I hurried on through the little town of Henderson to the levee, turning south on the levee road. I had realized about halfway down that I had not alerted a soul about my plans, which weren't without logistical challenge. I had no boat, no map, no real idea of exactly where in the huge swamp I should or could head. Don was the one who knew the swamp. Not I. I wanted it to be somewhere peaceful, away from the busy landings where this time of day the fishermen roar in with their catch and compare notes and hoot and holler and have a beer and otherwise exhibit the famous Cajun *joie de vivre*. As wonderful as that is to watch on a normal day, that's not what I wanted this day. Without a way to get *into* the swamp, I'd have to settle for one of the half-dozen landings.

Somehow fate lent a hand, and I thought of a friend who might help. When I pulled into his dirt drive, Greg Guirard, a wise and calm craw-fisherman whose yard is always full of work boats, was standing outside, as if waiting.

I told him my intention. He didn't hem or haw or otherwise delay. "I'll take you to a pretty place," he said. He then quickly—the sun was setting—backed my red truck up to his crawfishing skiff and trailer and we were off, to the nearest landing.

Greg knows the swamp the way a teenage girl knows the shopping mall. The boat hummed a short distance to Bayou Benoit, truly one of the magnificent spots on this old earth, especially at sundown. Without saying a word, Greg, a mountain of a man, stopped near a cypress grove and nodded. Then he disappeared. Not really, not literally, but he might as well have. That big, kind tree of a friend simply left me alone, not attempting, as some would have, to inject his own thoughts or ideas about the best way to fling your true love into the swampy waters. I have this memory of being all alone, transported as if by magic carpet to my task.

A human's ashes are not insignificant. I guess before Don's death and cremation I thought that they were. It takes a while to scoop them up a handful at a time and cast them like a net made of sand into the water. I was covered with residual death by the time the deed was done. Greg got us back to the landing.

The music had prepared me on the long drive down from North Mississippi to South Louisiana. Eight hours of music had stiffened my resolve and comforted me more than words or letters or grief books had been able to do. All those years of listening to Hank seemed to culminate in that one September day, when he sang the familiar songs but with new meaning and depth and the abiding comfort that comes in knowing you are lonely but not alone.

I wondered how many others had needed Hank in that same visceral way. How many others had let him weep and wail like a paid mourner at a rural funeral? Thousands, maybe millions. *But they love you so badly, for sharing their sorrows,* Kris wrote. They love you so badly. That day it was true for me. I loved Hank so badly.

Without music, life would be a mistake, Nietzsche said. I could add to that: Without music, death would be unbearable.

That saddest year of my life, 2009, Hank and his primal sound were invaluable friends. They eclipsed everything else—work, food, friends, family. It was both obsessive and necessary, this need to be blanketed by sound. I took no anti-depressants, no sleeping pills. I took heavy, daily doses of that music. Hank heals. And slowly, slowly, Hank rehung my moon.

A FEW FINAL THOUGHTS

*More and more mankind will discover that we have to
turn to poetry to interpret life for us, to console us, to
sustain us.*

— MATTHEW ARNOLD

Back to that box in the attic. The one with the hand-scrawled "Hank" on it. I spent the winter in Colorado dipping into that raggedy old cardboard box, fishing for inspiration and quotes. I found both, but mostly the former.

I was in Colorado Springs with a new husband, new to me anyway. He had been a husband before and lost a wife to a pulmonary aneurism eight years earlier. Hines Holt Hall and I married on December 23, 2010, and almost immediately afterwards headed west where he was to teach a history course at the Colorado College and I would work on this book. It was a grand way to start a marriage. Both of us immersed in our own worlds, yet ending up each evening in front of a fireplace, with books in our hands. On any given night, Hines might be re-reading *Candide*, while I read Hank Williams fan club newsletters or something of the sort. I began to think of our respective reading assignments as making us, brand new couple, what classmates signing your high school annual always called "well-rounded." That simply meant you could dribble a basketball and pass algebra. Well-rounded was a good thing.

I promised to tell you about my all-time favorite concert. This might be

the place. It was in January, 2010, at Nashville's Ryman Auditorium. Kris
Kristofferson stood alone with his guitar and harmonica on that storied
wooden stage. And he "sang up every song" we ever knew, in good voice
and with such an humble, grateful persona I left appreciating him more
than I already did. That night when Kris sang I sat beside Hines Hall for
the first time, and my life that had been so sad and bereft took a sudden
turn. Loving Hines was easier than anything I'll ever do again.

For so many reasons, Colorado was an ideal place for me to get started
on this book. I knew few folks in Colorado Springs, and distractions were
at a minimum. You could see Pikes' Peak from the window of the office
where I made camp, and snow capped it the entire four months we were
there. We would walk our three dogs each morning, then I'd settle in to
face the blank page. For once I enjoyed the agony of writing.

I believed that I had come to the correct point in my long nonfiction
career to let down my journalistic hair and, for once, write about a passion:
Hank Williams. On a recent visit to the Ogden Museum of Southern Art
in New Orleans, I was struck by the art, but mostly the words, of one Will
Henry Stevens (1881–1949), an Indiana painter whose work I had never
seen. Stevens one wrote this: "It has been my experience, and I think the
experience of all serious creative artists, if they have the good fortune of
working over a long period of time, gradually to depart from the rep-
resentation of surface appearance and to develop symbols expressive of
cosmic values. Art is based on emotional understanding . . ."

Emotional understanding. That was the secret of Hank's great genius,
why hew knew, for an instance, that the sky must be purple, not black
or blue or any other color. Why he knew that a heart was twice cold and
a mansion on a hill. He had not had the good fortune of working over a
long period of time. But Hank arrived early to that station of the cross.
His instincts were pitch-perfect. And I hoped my endurance, if nothing
else, made me worthy of writing about and understanding Hank, at least

in appreciation if not psychological insight.

The interviews stored in that old box were transcribed, from taped recordings, on a typewriter. Pat Grierson did the tedious job of transcribing, mailing Don duplicates of each and every interview. When you look at such type now it is instantly recognizable, at least to those of us old enough to remember typewriters. The spacing isn't perfect as on computer-generated pages; every now and again a letter jumps up higher than those around it as if to establish its superiority. The pages are like the Lascaux cave drawings in France, evidence of an earlier time.

The box became, for me, an object lessons as well as a source. So many of the conclusions those interviewed had come to in the early 1980s already had been proven wrong by the time I was writing. A few people, in less than prescient moments, even pronounced Hank Williams music dead. The box taught me, among other things, not to assume the dead are dead, especially if they have unique talent.

Hank is alive and well. He is alive and well for Helene Boudreaux, sitting on her porch swing in the Atchafalaya Swamp. He is alive for Jett Williams, living a fairytale existence in Tennessee. When Hank sang to me each night of this past year, he might as well have been in the room. He was alive for a man named Hank Woolsey, who told Pat Grierson how as a boy he jumped the fence in his Mobile back yard and got on the L&N Railroad tracks and walked shoeless the four or five miles to Mobile's Whiting Auditorium to hear his hero, Hank. "I watched the people around me as he sand, and when he would sing a happy song the people would be happy; a love song, I'd see people holding hands; when he sang a sad song, I'd see people cry and they didn't seem to be embarrassed about it . . ."

Hank is alive for my father, who keeps worn cassettes in his car the way a heart patient keeps nitroglycerin handy. After all these years, music remains an emotional staple, a basic mood group. I bought him a boom box a recent trip home because his old CD player had given up the ghost. A house without music is not only silent, but sad.

A blurb on the cover of my favorite book, Antoine de Saint-Exupery's *The Little Prince*, says: There are a few stories that in some way, in some degree, change the world forever for their readers. This is one.

I will say the same for Hank, only changing the medium. There are a few musicians that in some way, in some degree, change the world forever for their listeners.

Hank wrote, to quote the same Little Prince, about "matters of consequence," the verities, not things that do not matter next week. Hank wrote about loss and love, loneliness and guilt. Things that have always been around and always will be.

It takes a village to write a book, to prop up its author. Or that's the way it seems on days when you can't put your hand on the marvelous Whisperin' Bill Anderson quote, or you decide that your observations about a legend aren't worth a hoot in hell, or your computer goes haywire and along with it your thoughts. I want to thank friends in no particular order for their faith and interest in my one semi-marketable talent. I owe a debt to Sharon Thomason, Tony Salmon, Betty Douglass, Greg Guirard, Bill Garner, George Edmonson, Sherry Garner, Robert Khayat, Terry Martin, Ann Boutwell, Luke Hall, Barbara Minter, Anne Holtsford and Jimmy Johnson. Suzanne La Rosa and Randall Williams at NewSouth Books always gracefully bear the brunt of my procrastination and peculiar ways.

And special thanks are due my husband Hines Hall for sharing so many hours this past year listening to Hank, a learning experience, always, and pleasant, pleasant duty.

Somewhere in the Summer

Somewhere in the summer of one man's dream,
A guitar strummed his waiting,
And summered his need
With an old song
Lost in the tune of years humming
To fathomless seed,
As chords of desire swept by him,
As heedless as soundless drums
Beat on by tears.
It was his song he heard keeping rhythm
With time at his fingertrips,
As he marched his hand
To the tape's edge,
Though it said nothing
Of where in the world it had been,
As the man struck on the old strings,
And played to the room like a mindless mother
Who had married the moon.

— PAT GRIERSON, FROM
Somewhere a Tiger, PAON PRESS